The
Dinner Party
Cookbook

Karen Brown

 **Meadowbrook Press**
Distributed by Simon & Schuster
New York

Library of Congress Cataloging-in-Publication Data
Brown, Karen, 1952 Feb. 19-
    The dinner party cookbook/Karen Brown.
        p.   cm.
    Includes index.
    ISBN 0-88166-335-2 (Meadowbrook) — ISBN 0-671-31727-X (Simon &
    Schuster)
    1. Dinners and dining. 2. Menus. 3. Cookery.   I. Title.
TX737.B77   1999
642'.4—dc21   99-17771
                                                        CIP

Editor: Liya Lev Oertel
Copyeditor: Nancy Baldrica
Production Manager: Joe Gagne
Production Assistant: Danielle White
Cover Photo: StockFood America/Greene
Illustrations: Terri Mitchelson

Published by Meadowbrook Press, 5451 Smetana Drive; Minnetonka,
Minnesota 55343

www.meadowbrookpress.com

BOOK TRADE DISTRIBUTION by Simon & Schuster, a division of Simon and
Schuster, Inc., 1230 Avenue of the Americas, New York, NY 10020

03 02 01 00 99   10 9 8 7 6 5 4 3 2 1

Printed in the United States of America

Dedication

To my mother,
Betty Lancaster,
with love.

Acknowledgments

My special thanks go to the staff at Meadowbrook Press, especially publisher Bruce Lansky for his generosity of ideas and support, and my editor Liya Lev Oertel for her kind and creative guidance.

Contents

Special Occasions

Ethnic Themes

Introduction

A beautiful dinner party is one of the warmest and most gracious gifts you can give to your friends and family. And a dinner party is—or should be—more than just an assortment of foods and beverages. Every detail—from invitations to music to decorative touches—serves to enrich and complete the dining experience.

If you think that choosing, preparing, and serving the food is complicated enough, without having to also worry about ambiance, the *Dinner Party Cookbook* is just what you need. Owning this book is like having a professional party planner at your fingertips; you will find all the ingredients necessary to plan successful, fun, and delicious dinner parties—twenty-one complete menus, over a hundred recipes, and dozens of tips for theme decorating, table settings, background music, and more.

Whatever the occasion, we have the plan. Choose from a Formal Dinner when you want to impress, or an Academy Awards Supper when you're into fun and fantasy. Or how about a Romantic Dinner for Two with that special someone?

Many of the menus can be prepared before the party. And although all the recipes featured in each menu are included, you can save time and effort by purchasing some precooked and ready-to-serve items. The main thing is to get as much done ahead of time as possible, so you have time to relax, get ready, and enjoy your guests as they arrive. And if you have some last-minute sauces or stirring, simply bring the hors d'oeuvres (and the guests) into the kitchen so you and your guests can chat. I am sure you've noticed that the kitchen becomes a favorite gathering place at every party. The delicious smells and the intimate, informal atmosphere seem to act as magnets, no matter how much decorating and cleaning you may have done to the rest of the house or apartment.

Remember, even if you don't have the time or budget to implement all of our table decor suggestions, you can never go wrong with flowers and candles —lots of each. In fact, my favorite look is to have candles, candles, every-where (all the better to see you with, my dear, in the soft glow of candlelight). Place a votive candle at each place setting, or artfully group tapered candles of varying heights. However, never use scented candles or heavily fragrant flow-ers on a dinner table—nothing should compete or interfere with the aromas of the fabulous food you serve. And while a large flower arrangement is certain to be very decorative, make sure that your guests can see past the flowers to chat with their across-the-table neighbors.

Don't limit your decorating to the inside of the house. Create a warm and inviting entrance—string trees and shrubbery with white twinkle lights and line your sidewalk with lights and torches. If your party area overlooks the backyard, and if you happen to have a pool in that yard, float votive candles in tin pie pans in the pool. If you don't have a pool, you can get the same effect by floating candles and flower blossoms in wading pools. The result is really beautiful—especially at dusk.

Allow the decorating ideas in this book to spark your imagination and creativity as you pull together assorted odds and ends to create just the right effect. Improvise—the possibilities are endless:

- Candleholders: assorted jars, scooped-out fruits and vegetables, ashtrays, anything spray-painted or glitter-glued
- Centerpiece flora: large green leaves, eucalyptus, sheaves of straw or grain, feathers, groupings of fruits, vegetables or breads
- Table covers: colorful scarves, paper doilies, old bedspreads or quilts, fabric pieces from the remnant counter, even dish towels for a casual, whimsical look
- Ice buckets: decorative tubs or wading pools (outdoors), or your grandmother's samovar or favorite urn for a more formal setting

A Word about Wine

Gone are the days when strict wine-selection rules were de rigueur—you know, red with beef and white with fish or fowl. Contemporary gourmets now agree that anything goes, and don't forget to always offer a good sparkling water for the growing ranks of nondrinkers. You'll notice that each menu includes a few general wine suggestions. Read those recommendations, then please your own palate. However, you should still remember a few basics:

- Serve red wine at a cool room temperature in large-bowled glasses. Uncork the bottle an hour or so before pouring, allowing it to oxidize, which will enhance the flavor.
- Serve white and blush wines chilled—from the refrigerator or an ice bucket. Use narrow, tulip-bowled glasses.

- When pouring at the table, have an extra cloth napkin handy to wrap or tie around the bottle, saving you, your guests, and your tablecloth from random dripping.

When you want to extend the party, or when you simply want a four-star ending to your four-star evening, follow a lovely tradition from more civilized times—retire to the den or living room to sip a cup of steaming, full-bodied coffee or to cradle a snifter of warm brandy. To complete this experience, prepare a tray of coffee accompaniments:

- Selection of rich cognacs and liqueurs
- Dainty sugar cubes or coarse colored sugar
- Thick whipped cream
- Shaved chocolate
- Shakers of cinnamon and nutmeg

I hope that the recipes, decorating tips, and planning ideas in this book will be so helpful that you can accomplish one of the most important goals (I think) in hosting a dinner—to have as much fun at your party as your guests.

Enjoy!

Karen Brown

Karen Brown

Academy Awards Supper

The glamour. The glitz. The paparazzi and the adoring fans. Admit it. Some part of you wants to be a movie star—or at least look and act like one. Well, here's your chance. On this evening, let the everyday concerns and worries fall by the wayside, exchange the sweats for glamorous evening wear, and feel free to be someone other than yourself—are you a Marilyn or an Audrey? A Bing or a Cary? A star is born.

Menu

Goat Cheese Spread with Pita Crisps

Spinach Salad with Raspberry Vinaigrette

Scallops with Angel Hair Pasta and Sun-Dried Tomatoes

Flourless Chocolate and Raspberry Torte

Invitations

Send a telegram telling your guests, "You have been nominated to attend the awards dinner at . . . (place, date, time)." Ask them to come "Academy Awards Formal." Hopefully, you'll end up with men in ascots or tacky tuxedoes and women with feather boas and cigarette holders.

Decorations/Table Setting

- Arrange cocktail trays or a buffet table in your screening theater (TV room).
- Create a table centerpiece using a black top hat, white gloves, and black masks.
- Sprinkle glitter and sequins over the table, and decorate the walls with movie posters adorned with glittery tinsel.
- Set up a ballot table, and have guests fill them out before the show starts. Arrange the ballots around a lavishly wrapped gift that will be awarded to the guest who guessed the most winners correctly.

Music

Play songs from soundtracks nominated for Academy Awards.

Beverages

Serve martinis with hors d'oeuvres and a white Riesling with dinner.

Goat Cheese Spread with Pita Crisps

MAKES: 2 CUPS

8 ounces goat cheese, softened
3 ounces cream cheese, softened
1 clove garlic, minced
½ cup red bell pepper, minced

3 to 4 green onions, sliced
½ teaspoon salt
Pita crisps

1. Combine all ingredients, except pita crisps, in a food processor and blend until smooth.
2. Pour the cheese mixture into a decorative bowl and chill before serving.
3. Serve as a spread with pita crisps.

Spinach Salad with Raspberry Vinaigrette

MAKES: 6 SERVINGS, 1½ CUPS DRESSING

Spinach Salad:
1 pound fresh spinach leaves,
   washed

6 green onions, chopped
2 cups fresh strawberries, sliced

Raspberry Vinaigrette:
½ cup raspberry vinegar
½ cup olive oil

¼ cup sugar
½ teaspoon salt

1. Whisk together the vinaigrette ingredients; chill before serving.
2. Tear washed spinach leaves into a salad bowl.
3. Add green onions, and toss well.
4. Divide the spinach among six plates and top with sliced strawberries.
5. Drizzle each salad with raspberry vinaigrette.

Scallops with Angel Hair Pasta and Sun-Dried Tomatoes

MAKES: 6 SERVINGS

12 ounces angel hair pasta
4 tablespoons olive oil
1 clove garlic, minced
1 green bell pepper, cut into thin slices

1 cup prepared sun-dried tomatoes, sliced
¼ cup fresh basil, chopped
1 pound scallops
Salt and pepper, to taste
½ cup grated Parmesan cheese

1. In a large pot of boiling water, cook pasta according to package instructions, or until it is al dente. Drain.

2. While the pasta is cooking, heat olive oil in a large skillet over medium heat. Add garlic, green pepper, tomatoes, and basil, and sauté until the peppers are tender, but still crisp.

3. Add scallops and cook for 1 to 2 minutes on each side until the scallops are completely opaque.

4. Season with salt and pepper.

5. Divide the cooked pasta among six plates, spoon the scallop mixture on top, and sprinkle with Parmesan cheese. Serve immediately while still warm.

Tip: To prepare sun-dried tomatoes that have been dry-packed, soak them in a bowl of hot water for 20 to 30 minutes. Drain and dry well before using.

Flourless Chocolate and Raspberry Torte

MAKES: 8 SERVINGS

*8 ounces semisweet chocolate
squares, chopped*
⅓ cup water
8 eggs, separated
1 cup + ½ cup sugar

¼ teaspoon salt
½ teaspoon cream of tartar
2 pints whipping cream
1 teaspoon vanilla extract
2 pints fresh raspberries

1. Preheat the oven to 350 degrees.

2. Place chocolate pieces and water in top of a double boiler over hot water. Stir until the chocolate melts completely, then remove from heat.

3. Place egg yolks into a large bowl and beat with an electric mixer, gradually adding 1 cup sugar. Continue mixing until the mixture is thick, then add melted chocolate.

4. In separate bowl, beat egg whites on high speed. Add salt and cream of tartar and continue beating until almost stiff. Gently fold egg whites into the chocolate mixture and pour into two greased and floured 8-inch pans lined with wax paper.

5. Bake for 30 minutes, or until done. Cool (the cakes may fall in the center).

6. Whip cream with vanilla and remaining ½ cup sugar, beating until thick.

7. Invert one cake onto a serving plate. Top with a layer of whipped cream, and then a layer of raspberries.

8. Invert the second cake onto the raspberry layer, and top with remaining whipped cream, covering top and sides. Place remaining raspberries on top.

Chocolate makes a wonderful and delicious garnish to any dessert. To make your own chocolate curls, scrape the side of a square of cooking chocolate or a chocolate candy bar with a vegetable peeler, then decoratively arrange the curls on your cake. Another method, which works well for desserts served in glass dishes, such as mousses or parfaits, is chocolate piping. In fancy restaurants, you have probably seen beautifully arranged desserts on large plates with swirls of chocolate. Well, now you will be able to swirl with the best of them. Place a chocolate square in a heavy plastic bag and melt in the microwave. Cut a small hole in the corner of the bag and squeeze to "pipe" chocolate designs over the dessert or onto the serving plate. Let the chocolate harden before serving. Voilá!

Backyard Barbecue

It's summertime. And the cookin' is easy.

Everyone likes a barbecue—from the muckamucks to your mother-in-law. The simple and hearty fare has universal appeal and is appropriate for almost any sort of gathering—birthday, graduation, housewarming, or just because. Sitting outside in the fresh air, savoring juicy ribs, watching fireflies after dark . . . what's not to like?! Best of all, the preparations are simple, and most of the cooking is done outside—no slaving over a hot stove for this party.

Menu

Spinach and Cheese Spirals

Garlic Toast

Barbecued Spareribs

Potato-Vegetable Salad

Corn on the Cob

Watermelon Sorbet

Lemon Squares

Invitations

Glue printed invitations to burlap squares with fringed edges. Ask guests to dress "backyard casual" or specify western attire, if appropriate.

Decorations/Table Setting

- Give each guest a brightly colored bandanna to tie around his or her neck, and have extras to use as napkins at each place setting, along with tin camp dishes.
- Drape outdoor tables with burlap or checked tablecloths.
- For your centerpiece, fill cowboy boots with wildflowers or bunches of wheat tied with yarn.
- Fill Mason jars with wildflowers and distribute them throughout the party area.
- Use wagons or wheelbarrows as serving stations, and wooden cutting boards as trays, trivets, and servers.
- Serve snacks or food in large iron pots, or use the pots to hold silverware and napkins.
- Cover a patio floor with sawdust or hay.
- Light up the evening with kerosene lanterns. (Be careful to light up the *evening,* not the *hay!*)

Music

Set the mood with twangy country tunes from George Strait or Wynnona Judd. If you or a guest plays guitar, take requests for an after-dinner sing-along.

Beverages

Use Mason jars for drinks or have long-neck bottles of beer iced down. For dinner wine, serve a hearty red burgundy.

Spinach and Cheese Spirals

MAKES: 8 SERVINGS

6 ounces whipped cream cheese, softened

¼ cup sour cream

6 to 8 green onions, chopped

1 teaspoon garlic salt

10-ounce package frozen chopped spinach, thawed and drained

4 flour tortillas

¼ cup grated Parmesan cheese

1. In a mixing bowl, stir together cream cheese and sour cream until well blended. Add onions and garlic salt, then fold in spinach.

2. Wrap tortillas in slightly damp paper towels and heat in the microwave for 20 seconds so they will be pliable.

3. Lay tortillas out flat and spread a layer of spinach filling evenly over each. Tightly roll up each tortilla, wrap tightly with plastic wrap, and refrigerate for one hour or until ready to bake.

4. Preheat the oven to 400 degrees.

5. Remove the plastic wrap, cut each tortilla roll into ½- to ¾-inch slices, and place the round slices on a cookie sheet. Sprinkle with Parmesan cheese and bake for 6 to 7 minutes or until lightly browned.

Garlic Toast

MAKES: 8 SERVINGS

1 large loaf French bread, sliced

1 stick butter

1 teaspoon garlic, minced

1. Place bread slices on a cookie sheet and toast on one side under the oven broiler.

2. In a saucepan or a microwave-safe container, combine butter and garlic and heat over low heat or in microwave until melted.

3. Spread the butter mixture on untoasted sides of the bread and return the bread to the broiler, butter-side up, until golden. Serve immediately.

Tip: Before mincing garlic, sprinkle the garlic cloves with a little salt. The salt will absorb some of the garlic juice and keep the garlic from sticking to the knife.

Barbecued Spareribs

MAKES: 8 SERVINGS

1 cup ketchup
1 cup orange juice
⅓ cup honey
¼ cup soy sauce

2 cloves garlic, minced
1 teaspoon salt
½ teaspoon pepper
4 to 5 pounds pork spareribs

1. In a medium bowl, combine all ingredients except spareribs; mix well to make the marinade.

2. Arrange the ribs in a shallow pan and pour the marinade on top.

3. Cover the pan with a lid or aluminum foil and marinate for 8 hours or overnight.

4. Remove the ribs from the pan and place them on a preheated barbecue grill. Cook slowly, away from high heat, for about 20 to 30 minutes or until done, basting continually with remaining marinade. Serve with plenty of napkins.

Potato-Vegetable Salad

MAKES: 6 TO 8 SERVINGS

4 medium potatoes, cooked,
   peeled, and diced
Salt and pepper, to taste
1 cup mayonnaise
1 tablespoon prepared mustard
1 cup celery, chopped

1 cup green pepper, chopped
¼ cup carrots, shredded
½ cup sweet pickle relish
1 2-ounce jar diced pimientos
2 hard-boiled eggs, chopped

1. In large salad bowl, season potatoes with salt and pepper.

2. Combine mayonnaise and mustard and fold into potatoes, coating well.

3. Stir in remaining ingredients, adding more mayonnaise if desired.

4. Chill the salad well before serving.

Corn on the Cob

MAKES: 8 SERVINGS

8 medium ears of yellow corn　　*Butter*
Salt and pepper, to taste

1. Remove husks and corn silk, then cut tips off cobs.
2. Fill a large saucepan with unsalted water and bring to a boil.
3. Add the cleaned corn cobs, cover the saucepan, reduce heat to low, and simmer for about 10 minutes, or until corn is tender.
4. Drain the corn and serve warm with salt, pepper, and butter.

Watermelon Sorbet

MAKES: 6 SERVINGS

3 cups watermelon chunks,　　*2 tablespoons lemon juice*
　　seeded　　　　　　　　　　　*Thin watermelon wedges*
3 tablespoons sugar　　　　　　　*for garnish*

1. In a blender, mix together watermelon chunks, sugar, and lemon until slushy.
2. Pour the mixture into metal bowl and freeze for about 30 minutes.
3. Remove the bowl from the freezer and beat the mixture with an electric mixer. Repeat freezing/whipping process one or two more times before serving, until mixture reaches the desired consistency.
4. Pour the mixture into parfait glasses or dessert dishes and garnish with watermelon slices.

Lemon Squares

MAKES: 10 TO 12 SERVINGS

Crust Ingredients:

2 cups flour

2 sticks margarine, softened

½ cup powdered sugar

¼ teaspoon salt

Filling Ingredients:

4 eggs, lightly beaten

2 cups sugar

½ cup lemon juice

¼ cup flour

1 teaspoon baking powder

Topping Ingredients:

1 cup powdered sugar

1. Preheat the oven to 325 degrees.

2. Combine the crust ingredients and press into a 9-by-13-inch baking pan. Bake for 15 to 20 minutes or until golden brown.

3. While the crust bakes, make the filling: Combine beaten eggs with sugar and lemon juice. Sift together flour and baking powder and fold into the egg mixture. Mix well and pour over baked crust.

4. Return the pan to the oven and bake for 20 to 30 minutes.

5. Remove the pan from the oven and spread powdered sugar over the warm cake. Cool completely and cut into squares.

Since barbecues are so popular for Fourth of July celebrations, adjust your decorations and other details accordingly—instead of western/rustic, think red-white-and-blue patriotic. Decorate your dinner area with small flags and red, white, and blue streamers. Create centerpieces with red geraniums and blue cornflowers in white paper bags accented with firecrackers or sparklers. Serve a red, white, and blue dessert: Layer blueberries and strawberries with whipped cream in a glass trifle dish. Or, bake a white sheet cake in a rectangular pan and decorate the top to look like a flag. Have old-fashioned sack races and strike up the band with John Philip Sousa parade music.

Cocktails and Grazing

Pretty elegant.
Pretty smart.
And pretty easy.

That's the plan for this spiffy soiree you throw when you want your guests to mingle, munch, and meet each other. Although this is not a dinner party in the strictest sense of the term, the hearty array of hors d'oeuvres makes for a satisfying supper that gives your guests a chance to sample—and schmooze. And best of all, you can prepare everything ahead of time and join your guests without having to worry about serving, reheating, removing plates, and other such responsibilities that are definitely more work than play.

Menu

Pesto Cheesecake

Portobello Mushroom Bruschetta

Aioli Dip with Crudités

Smoked Salmon Crostini

Chocolate Truffles

Raspberry Tartlets

Invitations

Select good-quality cards with colored borders, and write your message with matching-colored pens.

Decorations/Table Settings

- Make a dramatic statement with color. Choose one shade that coordinates with the room and repeat that color in table cover, candles, and flowers.
- Cluster taper candles on mirrored trays. Accent with elegant vases filled with beautifully arranged flowers.
- Create interest with trays of varying heights, such as a footed cake stand or an elevated chafing dish. Or you can cheat by covering boxes or thick books with decorative cloths and using these improvised stands under your trays.
- Decorate trays with grapes or parsley spilling over the sides. (See sidebar for more food garnish ideas.)

Music

Provide a suitably sophisticated backdrop for the evening with sounds from Aaron Neville and Van Morrison. If you have a classical-loving group, the options are endless.

Beverages

Set up a makeshift bar at which guests can serve themselves. If offering mixed drinks, provide mixers, ice, lime wedges, lemon twists, olives, and stir sticks. Or, depending on your crowd, you may just want to offer a selection of white and red wines. Be sure to have plenty of sparkling water and soft drinks on hand for nondrinkers.

Pesto Cheesecake

MAKES: 20 SERVINGS

Crust Ingredients:

1 tablespoon butter, room temperature

¼ cup bread crumbs

2 teaspoons grated Parmesan cheese

Filling Ingredients:

16 ounces cream cheese

1 cup ricotta cheese

½ cup grated Parmesan cheese

¼ teaspoon salt

⅛ teaspoon cayenne pepper

3 large eggs

½ cup pesto (store-bought or homemade)

¼ cup pine nuts

Cocktail toasts

1. Preheat the oven to 325 degrees.

2. Butter bottom and sides of a 9-inch springform pan. Combine bread crumbs and 2 teaspoons Parmesan cheese and press the mixture into the pan.

3. To make the filling, use an electric mixer to beat the cheeses with salt and cayenne pepper, then add eggs, one at a time.

4. Transfer half the filling mixture into a separate bowl and add pesto to the remaining half; mix well.

5. Pour the pesto mixture into the pan, then top with reserved mixture. Smooth the top with a kitchen knife or wooden spoon, then sprinkle with pine nuts.

6. Bake for 45 minutes, or until set. Cool, cover, and refrigerate for 8 hours or overnight.

7. To serve, loosen the edges with knife, transfer to a tray, and surround with crisp toasts.

8. Provide decorative spreaders.

Portobello Mushroom Bruschetta

MAKES: 20 SLICES

Large loaf of heavy white bread
¼ cup + ¼ cup olive oil
1 pound portobello mushrooms,
* sliced*

3 to 4 green onions, chopped
2 garlic cloves, minced
1 cup dry white wine
Salt and pepper, to taste

1. Preheat the oven to 375 degrees.

2. Slice bread loaf in half lengthwise. Place both halves, cut side up, on a baking sheet and brush the tops with ¼ cup olive oil, dividing evenly between the halves.

3. Toast the bread in the oven for about 10 minutes or until the tops are golden brown. Remove from oven and slice each half into 10 thick slices.

4. In a large skillet over medium-low heat, warm the remaining ¼ cup olive oil, then add mushrooms, green onions, and garlic, sautéing about 5 minutes or until done.

5. Stir in wine and bring to a boil, then reduce heat and continue to stir for another 15 minutes.

6. Sprinkle the mushroom mixture with salt and pepper and spread over toasted bread. Serve warm or at room temperature.

Tip: If you have any leftover mushroom mixture, drain it and freeze it for future use—the mushrooms will make a wonderful addition to scrambled eggs and to most pasta sauces.

Aioli Dip with Crudités

MAKES: 12 SERVINGS

2 cups mayonnaise
1 teaspoon Dijon mustard
¼ teaspoon dried red pepper
2 + 2 tablespoons olive oil
6 garlic cloves, minced
10 to 20 cherry tomatoes
3 to 4 zucchini, sliced into rounds

1 pound carrots, peeled and
  sliced into sticks (or use whole
  baby carrots)
1 pound celery, sliced into sticks
2 green and 2 yellow bell
  peppers, sliced into strips
4 artichokes, boiled and chilled

1. In a large bowl combine mayonnaise, mustard, red pepper, and 2 table-spoons olive oil.

2. In a large skillet over medium-low heat, warm remaining 2 tablespoons olive oil, add garlic, and sauté for a few minutes to release the flavor of the garlic into the oil.

3. Stir the garlic and oil into the mayonnaise sauce, transfer the dip to a decorative bowl, and place on a platter surrounded by crudités (dipping vegetables).

Tip: Slice the vegetables a few hours before the party, place them in ice water, and store them in the refrigerator (up to 3 hours). Drain before serving. This process will make the vegetables crisper.

Smoked Salmon Crostini

MAKES: 12 SERVINGS

8 ounces whipped cream cheese
1 tablespoon sour cream
1 teaspoon lemon juice
⅓ cup chives, chopped
2 tablespoons capers

Cocktail toasts
1 pound smoked salmon,
  thinly sliced
Cut parsley sprigs

1. Combine cream cheese, sour cream, lemon juice, chives, and capers and blend well. Spread onto toasts.

2. Place salmon pieces on top of each toast and garnish each with a sprig of parsley.

Chocolate Truffles

MAKES: 24 TRUFFLES

16 ounces semisweet chocolate bits   *4 tablespoons butter*
¾ cup heavy cream   *½ cup cocoa powder*
¼ cup sweet liqueur or cognac   *½ cup powdered sugar*
  (Grand Marnier or Courvoisier)

1. In a large double boiler over medium heat stir together chocolate bits, cream, liqueur, and butter until everything melts and blends. Remove from heat and allow to cool.

2. Using an electric mixer, beat the chocolate mixture for about 10 minutes or until fluffy. Drop mixture by teaspoon onto a tray lined with wax paper and refrigerate.

3. Sift together cocoa and powdered sugar, roll each truffle in the mixture to coat evenly, then return to the refrigerator. Chill until serving time.

Raspberry Tartlets

MAKES: AS MUCH AS YOU WANT

Prepared French pastry shells or   *Raspberry preserves*
  mini pie crusts   *Fresh raspberries*
Prepared instant vanilla pudding

1. For each serving, fill a pastry shell to mid-level with pudding.

2. Cover the pudding with a thin layer of preserves, and top with fresh raspberries.

Turn ordinary into extraordinary—just a little effort goes a long way. You already know about garnishing your serving platters and dinner plates with sprigs of parsley and watercress; now try some of these artful accents:

- Radish Rosettes: *Wash large radishes and slice off one end. Use a paring knife to cut deep vertical gashes around the top, then slice thin layers down from the top to form petal shapes (scallops) all the way around. Immerse the radish in ice water for at least 1 hour, until petals open up.*

- Pickle Garnishes: *Select small pickles, and make several lengthwise slices. Leave slices attached at one end. Fan out slices.*

- Celery Fans: *Trim celery stalks and make narrow slits lengthwise from each end, meeting nearly in the center. Place the sliced stalks into a bowl of ice water for 1 hour, until ends begin to curl.*

Radish Rosette

Pickle Garnish

Celery Fan

Farmer's Harvest

When the farmers' fall harvest arrives and the smell of burning leaves is in the air, indulge in a bounty of the freshest fruits and vegetables in the marketplace: let the juice of the ripe tomatoes trickle down your chin, and inhale the heavenly aroma of apple cobbler made with freshly picked, tart apples. The back-to-nature trend is sweeping the country, as people are drawn to the simple, down-to-earth lifestyle of yesterday. With its fun, homespun decor and hearty, down-home food, this menu is a nod to our grandparents and to dinner tables of yore.

Menu

Spiced Cheese with Sesame Seed Crackers

Butternut Squash Soup

Juicy Glazed Baked Ham

Stewed Field Greens

Puréed Sweet Potatoes

Fresh Tomato Salad

Country Cornbread

Apple Cobbler

Invitations

Use harvest-themed notes bordered with cornucopias and/or vegetables. For a homey gathering, ask your guests to dress in denim.

Decorations/Table Setting

- Make your home inviting with baskets of pumpkins, corn, and fall berry branches nestled among bales of hay.
- Drape your table with an old-fashioned quilt and use coordinating napkins tied with raffia.
- For centerpieces, use plaid ribbon to accent produce containers filled with carrots, turnips, and radishes.

Music

Program your CD player with down-home favorites like Willie Nelson and Mary Chapin Carpenter. Who could resist such simple charm?

Beverages

Offer hot rum-spiked cider as a perfect accompaniment to the spiced cheese appetizer. For dinner, offer a chilled blush wine.

Spiced Cheese

MAKES 1 CUP

6 ounces sharp cheddar cheese,
  grated
3 ounces cream cheese, softened
2 teaspoons Dijon mustard

2 drops Tabasco sauce
¼ cup chives
Crackers

1. In a blender, combine cheeses with mustard and Tabasco; blend until smooth. Add chives and mix well.

2. Transfer the cheese mixture into a serving bowl and refrigerate until serving time.

3. Serve with sesame seed crackers (recipe follows). Provide decorative, vegetable-themed spreaders, if possible. (A wide variety of fun spreaders are readily available, and they add a fun touch to even the simplest dish.)

Sesame Seed Crackers

MAKES: 3 DOZEN

1 package dry yeast
1½ cups warm water
3½ cups flour
1 tablespoon salt

2 tablespoons vegetable oil + extra to
  brush rising dough
1 egg, beaten
½ cup sesame seeds

1. Combine yeast with water and let stand 5 minutes.

2. Sift flour and salt into mixture and stir in oil. Knead well for 5 minutes and transfer to a greased bowl.

3. Brush the top of the dough with extra oil and cover loosely. Allow to rise in a warm spot for 2 hours.

4. Preheat the oven to 450 degrees.

5. Turn the dough out onto a floured surface and roll to about ⅛-inch thickness.

6. Cut the dough with a 2-inch biscuit cutter and place each cracker onto a greased baking sheet.

7. Brush tops with beaten egg, then sprinkle with sesame seeds. Bake for about 7 to 9 minutes, or until golden brown. Allow to cool and crisp.

Butternut Squash Soup

MAKES: 6 SERVINGS

1 large butternut squash
Salt, to taste
½ stick butter
1 cup white onion, chopped

2 cans condensed chicken broth
1 cup heavy cream
Dash of nutmeg
Parsley or chives, chopped, for garnish

1. Bake a large whole squash in a 400-degree oven for 1 hour, or until tender.

2. Cool the squash slightly, then scoop out pulp, discarding seeds. Sprinkle the pulp with salt.

3. In a large saucepan, melt butter over low heat; add onion and sauté until tender.

4. In a blender, combine squash with 1 can of broth; blend on high speed until smooth.

5. Place the squash mixture and remaining broth in the pan with sautéed onion; stir in cream.

6. Heat the soup, stirring regularly, until thoroughly heated.

7. Ladle the soup into serving bowls and sprinkle with nutmeg.

Tip: Sprinkle chopped parsley or chopped chives on top of the soup, for garnish.

Juicy Glazed Baked Ham

MAKES 12 SERVINGS

6- to 8-pound fully cooked,
boneless ham
Whole cloves
1 cup brown sugar

½ cup dark corn syrup
2 tablespoons prepared mustard
1 teaspoon lemon juice

1. Preheat the oven to 325 degrees.
2. Place ham into a roasting pan and insert meat thermometer. Bake for 2 to 2½ hours, or until thermometer reaches 130 degrees.
3. Remove the pan from the oven and remove the thermometer. Make shallow, diagonal, crisscross cuts in the fat along the top of the ham, forming a grid-like pattern. Push a whole clove into each diamond shape.
4. Mix together brown sugar, corn syrup, mustard, and lemon juice and pour on top of ham.
5. Adjust the oven temperature to 400 degrees and return ham to the oven for 10 minutes, or until glaze is golden.
6. Slice the ham into thick, hearty slices for serving.

Stewed Field Greens

MAKES: 8 SERVINGS

3 pounds fresh mustard or
turnip greens

½ pound salt pork
Salt and pepper, to taste

1. Wash greens, removing stems. Place in a large pot and cover with boiling water; add salt pork.
2. Cover, bring to a simmer, and cook for about 1 hour, or until tender.
3. Season with salt and pepper, to taste.

Puréed Sweet Potatoes

MAKES: 8 SERVINGS

6 medium sweet potatoes
Salt, to taste
1 teaspoon cinnamon

½ teaspoon nutmeg
½ cup butter, softened
¾ cup heavy cream

1. Preheat the oven to 350 degrees.
2. Thoroughly scrub the potatoes and pierce them with a fork or a knife.
3. Wrap the potatoes in aluminum foil and bake for 1 hour, or until soft. Cool, peel, and place in a large mixing bowl.
4. Use an electric mixer to beat the potatoes until smooth, then stir in spices, butter, and cream.
5. Turn the potato mixture into a baking dish and bake for 30 to 40 minutes, or until heated through.

Fresh Tomato Salad

MAKES: 6 SERVINGS

6 ripe tomatoes
1 sweet red onion, sliced into
    thin circles
¼ cup fresh basil, chopped

¼ cup olive oil
1 teaspoon red wine vinegar
Salt and pepper, to taste

1. Chop tomatoes into bite-sized wedges.
2. Toss with remaining ingredients.

Country Cornbread

MAKES 12 SERVINGS

2 eggs
1 cup milk
3 tablespoons butter, melted
1 cup flour
1 cup yellow cornmeal

4 teaspoons baking powder
2 teaspoons sugar
1 teaspoon salt
1 10-ounce can cream-style corn

1. Preheat the oven to 400 degrees.

2. In a large mixing bowl, beat together eggs, milk, and butter.

3. Sift dry ingredients into the egg mixture; blend well.

4. Fold in cream-style corn.

5. Pour the batter into a greased 9-by-13-inch baking dish and bake for 30 minutes.

6. Cut and serve while warm.

Mmm. . . . Fill the air with wonderful aromas with this easy stovetop scent: In a small pot, combine apple cider with cloves, cinnamon sticks, and orange peel; simmer on the back burner all evening. (Make sure to always keep liquid in the pan; as the cider boils out, you may have to add more during the evening to prevent scorching.) Experiment with other combinations, including lemonade with peppermint, or orange juice with chopped ginger. Any and all of these combinations make easy, economical—and exquisite—potpourri.

Apple Cobbler

MAKES: 6 SERVINGS

Filling Ingredients:

5 cups tart baking apples, peeled and sliced

2 tablespoons lemon juice

2 tablespoons flour

¾ cup sugar

1 teaspoon cinnamon

3 tablespoons butter

Crust Ingredients:

½ cup flour

1 teaspoon baking powder

¼ teaspoon salt

½ cup sugar

2 tablespoons butter, softened

1 egg, beaten

Ice cream

1. Preheat the oven to 375 degrees.

2. To make the filling, place apples in a large mixing bowl and sprinkle with lemon juice.

3. Stir in flour, sugar, and cinnamon, and turn everything into an 8-by-8-inch baking pan. Dot with butter.

4. In a separate bowl, sift together flour, baking powder, salt, and sugar.

5. Add butter and egg; mix well.

6. Drop batter by large spoonful onto the apple mixture; spread as evenly as possible with the back of the spoon. The raw batter will not cover the apples completely, but it will spread during baking.

7. Bake for 40 minutes. Serve warm with ice cream.

Formal Dinner

Most of us have had people over for casual dinners—from ordering a pizza or Chinese food to throwing together some pasta and a salad. Such gatherings are simple and relatively stress-free. However, once in a while, whatever the celebration—a birthday, graduation, or special achievement—it's time to pull out all the stops. So, dust off your good china, polish the silver, air out the crisp white linen, and bring down the crystal from the top shelf. There's something about a dimly lit room, with the scent of freshly cut flowers and the air of breathless anticipation—when you're waiting for the first guest to arrive, and you know that everything is perfect. And we've planned an evening so fabulous and festive, your guests'll surely be toasting you by the time the night is over.

Menu

Pesto Pinwheels

Arugula and Orange Salad

Salmon en Croute with Dill Sauce

Wild Rice with Pine Nuts

Steamed Asparagus with Butter Sauce

Dinner Rolls with Herbed Butter

Crème Brûlé

Invitations

For a formal look, write the invitation information with a black fountain pen on traditional cream-colored stock. For a festive touch, glue some metallic confetti onto the invitations or inside the envelopes.

Decorations/Table Setting

- For classic elegance, fill a crystal bowl with cut roses and flank the bowl with two silver candlesticks.
- If you want to be more inventive, fill an array of small crystal vases with baby's breath and Queen Anne's lace, and set individual votive candles at each place setting.
- Use your best china, silver, and linens—of course!

Music

Choose from among classical favorites, such as Vivaldi, Chopin's piano concertos (my personal favorite), or Bach.

Beverages

Serve a California chardonnay and a first-rate champagne to toast your celebratory event.

Pesto Pinwheels

MAKES: 8 SERVINGS

1 sheet frozen puff pastry, thawed　*½ cup grated Parmesan cheese*
Flour　*1 egg, beaten with 1 teaspoon water*
⅛ cup pesto　*Fresh basil for garnish*

1. Preheat the oven to 400 degrees.

2. Roll out pastry on a floured surface to a 14-by-11-inch rectangle. Spread pesto evenly over the entire surface, then sprinkle with cheese.

3. Lift edge of dough on the long side and roll up. Cut the pastry roll into ½-inch thick slices and lay the slices flat on a greased cookie sheet.

4. Brush the tops of the rolls with the egg mixture, place in the oven, and bake for 8 to 10 minutes, or until golden brown.

5. Arrange the pinwheels on a serving platter and garnish with fresh basil. Serve warm or at room temperature.

Arugula and Orange Salad

MAKES: 8 SERVINGS

3 large bunches arugula, torn　*½ cup olive oil*
　into bite-sized pieces　*3 tablespoons red wine vinegar*
2 large oranges, peeled and cut　*½ teaspoon garlic, minced*
　into bite-sized pieces

1. Combine arugula and orange pieces in a large salad bowl.

2. In a separate bowl, whisk together oil, vinegar, and garlic; pour over greens and fruit.

3. Toss well and serve.

Tip: If you serve the salad on individual plates, as opposed to having the guests help themselves, garnish each plate with a long strip of orange peel.

Salmon en Croute with Dill Sauce

MAKES: 8 SERVINGS

Sauce Ingredients:

1 pint sour cream

¼ cup Dijon mustard

½ cup fresh dill, chopped

Fish Ingredients:

2 cups water

2 pounds salmon fillets

¼ cup butter

1 cup onions, chopped

2 cups mushrooms, sliced

Dash of salt and pepper

1 17-ounce package frozen

puff pastry, thawed

1. Since the sauce should be chilled before serving, prepare it before you begin the fish: Combine sour cream, mustard, and dill; mix well. Refrigerate until ready to serve.

2. Preheat the oven to 400 degrees.

3. In a large skillet, bring water to a boil, then turn down heat to low and add salmon; cook until the salmon flakes, about 10 minutes.

4. Remove the salmon from the pan with a slotted spoon or spatula; pour off the water. Divide the fish into two equal pieces; set aside.

5. In a large skillet over low heat, melt butter; add onions and cook for about 5 minutes, then add mushrooms and simmer until tender. Sprinkle with salt and pepper and remove from heat.

6. Roll out a sheet of pastry and place half the fish on top. Spread half of the sautéed onions and mushrooms, including the butter, over salmon pieces. Fold sides of pastry over fish, sealing at the top.

7. Repeat with remaining pastry and fish.

8. Place both fish bundles on a greased cookie sheet. Put in the oven and bake for about 30 minutes, or until the dough is golden brown. Let the bundles set for a minute, then slice each one into four sections.

9. Serve with chilled sauce.

Wild Rice with Pine Nuts

MAKES: 8 SERVINGS

2 cups wild rice
4 cups chicken stock
2 cups water

2 teaspoons salt
6 to 8 green onions, chopped
2 cups pine nuts

1. Place rice, stock, water, and salt in a large saucepan; bring to a boil.

2. Lower the heat to simmer, then cover the saucepan and cook for 30 to 45 minutes, stirring occasionally, until most of the liquid is absorbed and the rice is tender.

3. Remove from heat and stir in onions and pine nuts.

Steamed Asparagus with Butter Sauce

MAKES: 8 SERVINGS

1 pound asparagus
½ cup butter

1 teaspoon lemon juice
¼ teaspoon salt

1. Cut off the tough white ends of each asparagus spear. Place the asparagus spears in a steamer over boiling salted water.

2. Cook uncovered for 15 to 20 minutes, or until tender. Drain.

3. In a microwave, combine remaining ingredients and heat until butter melts. Pour over asparagus.

Dinner Rolls

MAKES: ABOUT 16 ROLLS

½ cup milk
½ cup water
¼ cup butter
3 tablespoons sugar
1 package dry yeast

¼ cup warm water
1 egg, beaten
3¼ cups flour
1 teaspoon salt

1. In a medium saucepan, combine milk, water, butter, and sugar. Bring to a boil over medium to high heat, stirring frequently. Remove from heat and cool.

2. Mix yeast with warm water and add to the milk mixture.

3. Stir in egg.

4. Sift together flour and salt and combine with the milk-and-yeast mixture to form dough. Turn the dough out onto a floured surface and knead until smooth.

5. Place the dough into a large buttered bowl, cover with wax paper, and refrigerate overnight.

6. Several hours before baking, roll out the dough on a floured surface to about ½-inch thick; cut with 2-inch round cutters. Place the rolls on a greased baking pan and let them rise in a warm place for about 2 hours.

7. Preheat the oven to 400 degrees.

8. Bake the rolls for 15 to 20 minutes, or until golden brown. Serve warm with herbed butter (recipe follows).

Herbed Butter

MAKES: ½ CUP BUTTER

1 stick butter, softened

1 teaspoon fresh chives, chopped
1 tablespoon fresh tarragon, chopped

1. Cream together all ingredients.

2. Arrange decoratively in a serving container and chill until serving.

Crème Brûlé

MAKES: 6 SERVINGS

2 cups heavy cream
5 egg yolks

½ cup + 6 tablespoons granulated
sugar
1 teaspoon vanilla extract

1. Preheat the oven to 400 degrees.

2. In a saucepan, heat cream just to boiling.

3. In a separate bowl, beat egg yolks with ½ cup sugar until thick. Stir cream into eggs and add vanilla; mix well.

4. Place 6 ½-cup ramekins (small dishes used for baking and serving) in a large shallow baking pan. Pour the mixture into the ramekins. Pour water into the pan, about halfway up the ramekins' sides.

5. Bake for 15 to 20 minutes, or until the custard is firm on top. Chill for several hours, until the custard is firm.

6. Sprinkle 1 tablespoon of sugar evenly across the top of each custard; place the custards on a baking sheet and brown under a preheated broiler for 2 to 3 minutes, or until the top is caramelized and crisp. Cool before serving.

Tip: You can serve these desserts in the ramekins or turn them out onto decorated plates (see sidebar). To turn them out, slide a dinner knife around the edges, place the serving plate on top, and gently flip over.

Serve your very elegant desserts on plates of decoratively swirled sauces. All you need are two bottles of ice cream toppings. Pour a raspberry sauce onto a plate, then draw circles on top with a vanilla sauce. (Or use a chocolate and caramel combination.) Swirl a kitchen knife through the sauces to make beautiful designs.

Late-Night Buffet

Opening night at the opera.
The season's finale at the symphony.
A fabulous exhibit at the museum.

   You'll hit a high note when you invite friends over for a bite after the event. And as you pull this simply stunning spread out of the refrigerator, shrug effortlessly and say, "Oh, it was nothing."

Menu

Olive-Tomato Spread with Baguettes

Mixed Greens with Goat Cheese and Walnuts

Bulgur Salad

Cold Roasted Herb Chicken

Strawberries Sabayon

Invitations

Make copies of the event ticket and glue them to festive cards. Write the invitation information underneath. Ask your guests to RSVP by phone so you can be sure your seats are filled! Plan to invite an extra couple whom you may run into that evening.

Decorations/Table Setting

- Hang symphony/opera/ballet posters.
- Use toy musical instruments, old theater playbills, or a collection of masks—all nestled within flowers—for the buffet tables and seating area.
- Light lots of candles to create an intimate and glamorous atmosphere.

Music

Play show-tune soundtracks or music from the performance you've just attended.

Beverages

Have bottles of a nice pinot blanc chilled and ready to serve.

Olive-Tomato Spread with Baguette

MAKES: 8 SERVINGS

3 ripe roma tomatoes, finely
   chopped
½ cup black olives, finely sliced
¼ cup red onion, minced
¼ cup fresh basil, finely chopped

2 tablespoons olive oil
1 tablespoon red wine vinegar
Sprig of fresh basil for garnish
Toasted baguettes

1. Combine vegetables with basil, oil, and vinegar; mix gently, but thoroughly.
2. Transfer the spread to a serving dish and chill until serving.
3. Garnish with a sprig of fresh basil.
4. Serve with warm, toasted baguettes.

Tip: To make sure the toast is nice and warm when serving, slice the baguettes ahead of time and keep them in a plastic bag until ready to serve. Then simply pop them into the toaster. To make the last minute preparations even simpler, you can place the sliced baguettes into the toaster before you leave, and then simply press the lever when ready to serve. (Make sure, however, that the bread doesn't sit out too long, or it will get dry.)

Oil-based spreads or dipping sauces for breads—such as the tantalizing tomato-olive variation offered here—are a sensational, and surprisingly simple, food trend. If you like our recipe, you may also want to create your own oil-and-herb combination. Following are a few of my favorites:

• Prosciutto and Gruyere on sesame seed rolls

• Eggplant and feta on pita bread

• Mushrooms and goat cheese on flatbread

Voilá—an awesome appetizer, or a luscious lunch.

Mixed Greens with Goat Cheese and Walnuts

MAKES: 6 SERVINGS

2 bunches green leaf lettuce
1 bunch watercress
1 cup walnut halves
¼ pound goat cheese, crumbled

½ cup vegetable oil
2 tablespoons red wine vinegar
1 teaspoon sugar

1. Wash lettuce and remove stems from watercress; tear the greens into bite-size pieces and place in a large salad bowl with walnuts and cheese. Refrigerate until needed.

2. In a separate bowl, mix together oil, vinegar, and sugar. Refrigerate until needed.

3. Just before serving, pour the dressing over the salad and toss well.

Bulgur Salad

MAKES: 6 SERVINGS

2 cups chicken broth
1 cup bulgur (cracked wheat)
⅓ cup lemon juice
¼ cup olive oil
1 teaspoon garlic, minced

1 cup celery, chopped
1 cup onion, chopped
1 cup cucumber, chopped
2 tomatoes, finely chopped

1. In a large saucepan, bring broth to a boil; stir in bulgur. Cover, lower heat to simmer, and cook for about 15 minutes, or until liquid is absorbed.

2. Pour bulgur into a large salad bowl and allow to cool.

3. Stir in lemon juice, olive oil and garlic, then add remaining ingredients and toss well. Refrigerate until serving time.

Cold Roasted Herb Chicken

MAKES: 6 SERVINGS

3 pounds roasting chicken, trussed
¼ pound butter, melted
Salt and pepper, to taste
½ cup tarragon

½ cup basil, chopped
1 teaspoon garlic, minced
Fresh basil, for garnish

1. Preheat the oven to 375 degrees.

2. Place the chicken into a shallow roasting pan.

3. Brush the chicken with melted butter, then sprinkle with salt, pepper, half the tarragon, and half the basil. Mix together minced garlic with the remaining butter and herbs; brush inside the chicken.

4. Bake for about 45 minutes, or until the chicken is almost done. The juices should run clear and the drumstick should move easily in its socket.

5. Increase heat to 400 degrees and bake for another 15 minutes to brown. Cool.

6. Slice the chicken into serving pieces and arrange on a serving platter with fresh basil. Wrap with plastic wrap and refrigerate until serving.

Strawberries Sabayon

MAKES: 6 SERVINGS

4 egg yolks
¾ cup sugar
1 cup whipping cream

¼ cup Grand Marnier liqueur
2 pints strawberries, sliced

1. In a large mixing bowl, combine egg yolks and sugar; beat with an electric mixer until smooth.

2. Transfer the egg mixture to the top of double boiler; cook over low heat until thickened, stirring continuously, about 10 minutes. Remove from heat and allow to cool.

3. In a separate bowl, use a mixer to whip cream until thick; stir in liqueur.

4. Fold the cream into the custard mixture.

5. Fold in strawberries; reserve a few strawberries for garnish.

6. Spoon the mixture into glass parfait dishes and refrigerate until serving.

Happy Housewarming

Ah, the trials and tribulations of moving. Tripping over boxes. Trying to find your clothes in the morning. Crates and cartons masquerading as end tables. But when the disarray is under control and you have established some semblance of order, it's time to celebrate. And how better to bask in the warmth of your new abode than with the good cheer of friends and the aromas of a delicious dinner. This menu (not to mention your finely honed decorating skills) should earn you standing ovations, rave reviews, and never-ending accolades.

Menu

Spinach and Oyster Crostini

Tomatoes with Mozzarella

Roast Pork Loin with Cherry Relish

Baked Green Rice

Glazed Carrots

Swiss Chard

Praline Cheesecake

Invitations

Use informal notes with a photo of your new home, or maybe a "change of address" card motif.

Decorations/Table Setting

- If you've redecorated, display plenty of "before and after" photos.
- Stuff large moving boxes with gaily colored tissue paper.
- For a centerpiece, fill an empty paint can with bright flowers of the season, and nestle hammers and paintbrushes among the flowers.
- Wrap large jars with colored cellophane (leave the tops open) and use them as candle holders for a colorful glow.

Music

Choose smooth instrumentals from the Windham Hill artists—the *Piano Sampler II* and *Windham Hill Retrospective* are especially good.

Beverages

Choose a blush wine to enhance the pork and other menu items.

Spinach and Oyster Crostini

MAKES: 6 TO 8 SERVINGS

10-ounce package frozen
   chopped spinach
Olive oil
1 clove garlic, minced
¼ cup grated Parmesan cheese

1 tablespoon lemon juice
Salt and pepper, to taste
1 to 2 dozen small toasts
8-ounce can oysters, drained

1. Preheat the oven to 350 degrees.

2. Cook spinach in the microwave according to package directions; drain.

3. In a skillet, heat olive oil; add garlic and sauté for a few minutes to release the flavor.

4. Add cooked spinach to the garlic, then fold in Parmesan cheese and lemon juice. Remove from heat.

5. Season with salt and pepper, to taste.

6. Place small toasts on a baking sheet. Place a spoonful of spinach mixture on each toast, then top each one with an oyster. Drizzle with olive oil.

7. Bake for 6 to 7 minutes, or until heated through. Serve warm.

Tomatoes with Mozzarella

MAKES: 6 SERVINGS

6 large ripe tomatoes
1 pound mozzarella cheese
⅓ cup olive oil

⅛ cup basil, chopped
Salt and pepper

1. Cut tomatoes and mozzarella into ½-inch-thick slices; layer on individual plates.

2. Drizzle with olive oil, then sprinkle with basil, salt, and pepper.

Roast Pork Loin

MAKES: 8 SERVINGS

3½ pounds pork tenderloin
½ cup soy sauce
½ cup sherry

2 cloves garlic, minced
1 teaspoon ground ginger
1 teaspoon dry mustard

1. Place pork tenderloin in a shallow baking pan.

2. Combine remaining ingredients and pour over meat; marinate for several hours in the refrigerator, turning once.

3. Preheat the oven to 325 degrees.

4. Insert meat thermometer and bake uncovered for 45 to 60 minutes, until thermometer registers 165 degrees. Baste frequently with marinade.

5. Allow to cool a few minutes before slicing into medallions. Serve with cherry relish on the side (recipe follows).

Cherry Relish

MAKES: 2 CUPS

½ cup bell pepper, chopped
½ cup onion, chopped
2 tablespoons vinegar

½ cup cherry preserves
½ cup dried cherries (if not available, can double the amount of preserves)

1. Mix together all ingredients. Chill to blend flavors.

2. Serve at room temperature.

Tip: This relish can be made 1 hour to one day ahead of time.

If you still have a few small jobs that need doing around the house—such as hanging pictures or hooking up electronics—turn your dinner party into a "working" housewarming. Ask your guests to come an hour earlier, ready to roll up their sleeves. Take Polaroids of them at work, then display the photos on your refrigerator as your "Friends' Hall of Fame."

Baked Green Rice

*2 cups long-grain rice, cooked to
  yield 4 cups*
½ cup Swiss cheese, grated
½ cup parsley, chopped
½ cup onion, chopped
¼ clove garlic, minced

½ teaspoon salt
¼ teaspoon pepper
1 cup milk
1 egg, beaten
2 tablespoons butter, melted

1. Preheat the oven to 350 degrees.
2. In a large mixing bowl, combine cooked rice with cheese, parsley, onion, garlic, and spices.
3. In a separate bowl, combine milk, egg, and butter; mix well and stir into the rice mixture.
4. Pour everything into a greased casserole, cover, and bake for 1 hour.

Glazed Carrots

MAKES: 6 SERVINGS

*1 pound carrots, peeled and
  chopped*
4 tablespoons butter

4 tablespoons brown sugar
2 teaspoons lemon juice
Salt, to taste

1. Place carrots in boiling water and cook 15 to 20 minutes or until tender.
2. Drain and return to pan.
3. Stir in remaining ingredients and cook over low heat until thoroughly combined. Serve warm.

Swiss Chard

MAKES: 6 SERVINGS

*2 pounds Swiss chard leaves,
   stems removed*
4 strips bacon

1 cup onion, chopped
Salt and pepper, to taste

1. In a saucepan, bring water to a boil; add chard, bacon, and onion.
2. Lower heat, cover, and simmer for 15 to 20 minutes, or until tender. Season with salt and pepper.

Praline Cheesecake

MAKES: 10 SERVINGS

1 cup graham cracker crumbs
3 tablespoons sugar
3 tablespoons butter, melted
*1½ pounds cream cheese,
   softened*
1½ cups brown sugar

3 eggs
2 tablespoons flour
1 teaspoon cinnamon
1 cup pecans, chopped
1 teaspoon vanilla
Cinnamon and pecans for decoration

1. Preheat the oven to 350 degrees.
2. Mix together graham cracker crumbs, sugar, and butter; press into the bottom of an 8-inch springform pan. Bake for 10 minutes, or until browned. Cool in the pan.
3. In a large mixing bowl, cream together cream cheese and brown sugar with an electric mixer. Add eggs, one at a time.
4. Mix in flour, cinnamon, pecans, and vanilla; pour everything over the cooled graham cracker crust.
5. Bake for 50 to 60 minutes, or until filling is firm. Cool, then remove pan and transfer the cake to a serving plate. Chill. Lightly dust with cinnamon and decorate with pecans before serving.

New Year's Eve

New Year's Eve. A time for reviewing, renewing, and rejoicing. Since it only comes one night a year, break out the champagne and give each guest an opportunity to do a little toasting and boasting. Go around the table and have each guest share the most outstanding things that happened in their lives over the past year—and their resolutions for the next one. According to tradition, how you meet the New Year will determine how the rest of the year will go. So be sure that you meet the year with something sparkly in your glass, something delicious in your mouth, and some good friends to surround you.

Menu

Tomato-Basil Bruschetta

Lobster Bisque

Osso Bucco

Risotto with Porcini Mushrooms

Roasted Zucchini

Tiramisu

Invitations

Use stark black-and-white paper and ink. Ask your guests to dress up in black and white.

Decorations/Table Setting

Create a dramatic black-and-white setting:

- Cover small boxes with black paper and line them with black tissue paper. Spray branch limbs with white paint and place the branches into the boxes. These will make elegant and festive decorative items for your party room.

- Use white china with sleek black runners.

- For centerpieces, fill vases with minimalist white flowers (or use white potted flowers). Wrap the vases or pots with white tissue paper, and trim with black ribbon.

- Light black-and-white sparkler candles at midnight, in time for the toasts.

Music

According to New Year's tradition, play sophisticated big band sounds from Benny Goodman and Glen Miller.

Beverages

Champagne, champagne, and more champagne. (Okay, maybe switch to a nice cabernet sauvignon at dinnertime.)

Tomato-Basil Bruschetta

MAKES: 6 SERVINGS

1 loaf French bread, thickly sliced
3 garlic cloves, sliced
½ cup olive oil

3 ripe tomatoes, finely chopped
3 tablespoons basil, chopped
Salt and pepper, to taste

1. Place bread slices on a cookie sheet and toast under a preheated broiler for 2 to 3 minutes or until golden and crisp.

2. Remove from oven. Rub each slice with garlic cloves, then brush with olive oil. Divide the slices among individual plates.

3. Spoon tomatoes onto each slice; sprinkle with basil, salt, and pepper.

Lobster Bisque

MAKES: 6 SERVINGS

½ cup butter
1 cup shallots, chopped
1 cup celery, chopped
1 clove garlic, minced
⅓ cup flour

6 cups cream
3 cups cooked lobster pieces
1 bay leaf
Dash of dry sherry
Freshly ground black pepper, to taste

1. In a large saucepan, melt butter; stir in shallots, celery, and garlic. Sauté for several minutes until vegetables are soft. Stir in flour (to thicken the soup), then add cream, stirring constantly.

2. Add lobster and bay leaf; cook over low heat, continuing to stir, for 20 minutes, or until heated through.

3. Remove bay leaf, then stir in sherry. Ladle the soup into bowls; sprinkle with freshly ground black pepper.

Osso Bucco

MAKES: 6 SERVINGS

6 veal shanks, sliced into 2-inch-
   thick pieces
¾ cup flour
1 teaspoon salt
½ teaspoon pepper
¼ cup olive oil
2 cups onion, chopped

2 cups celery, chopped
2 cloves garlic, minced
1½ cups dry white wine
1½ cups stewed tomatoes
2 teaspoons fresh basil, chopped
1 bay leaf

1. Dredge veal chunks in a mixture of flour, salt, and pepper; coat on all sides.

2. In a large saucepan, heat olive oil over medium heat.

3. Add veal to the hot oil and cook, turning occasionally, until the meat is evenly browned. Remove veal to a warmed platter.

4. Add onions, celery, and garlic to the saucepan and sauté for a few minutes, then add remaining ingredients.

5. Bring to a boil, stirring constantly.

6. Add veal and lower heat.

7. Cover and simmer for about 2 hours. Remove bay leaf before serving.

Black-eyed peas. Herring. Cabbage. Pork. In many parts of the country, these are traditional dishes served at New Year's for good luck. In the South, for instance, black-eyed peas are served as a dip: Drain 2 1-pound cans of black-eyed peas and mix with ¾ cup salad oil, ¼ cup wine vinegar, ¼ cup sliced red onion, 1 4-ounce can chopped green chilies, 1 teaspoon minced garlic, and salt and pepper, to taste. Chill and serve with crackers. This dish may not seem appropriate for an elegant champagne dinner, but anything that may help increase your luck for the coming year can only be good. Cheers!

Risotto with Porcini Mushrooms

MAKES: 6 SERVINGS

6 cups chicken broth
¼ cup olive oil
1 clove garlic, minced
1 small onion, minced
1 cup porcini mushrooms, sliced

2 cups arborio rice
1 cup dry white wine
½ cup freshly grated
*   Parmesan cheese*
Salt and pepper, to taste

1. In a medium saucepan, bring broth to a boil, then lower heat to a simmer. Keep warm on low heat.

2. In a large saucepan, heat olive oil, then add garlic, onion, and mushrooms; sauté for a few minutes until soft.

3. Add rice; stir well.

4. Increase heat, then stir in wine.

5. Add hot broth, 1 cup at a time, stirring until each cup is completely absorbed before adding another. Continue cooking and stirring for a few minutes until rice is al dente (firm to the bite). Remove pan from heat.

6. Fold in Parmesan cheese, then sprinkle with salt and pepper.

Roasted Zucchini

MAKES: 6 SERVINGS

3 large zucchini
2 tablespoons olive oil

Salt and pepper, to taste

1. Preheat the oven to 375 degrees.

2. Remove stems from zucchini; slice each zucchini lengthwise.

3. Place the zucchini halves into a shallow baking dish, cut side up, and drizzle with olive oil, then season with salt and pepper, to taste.

4. Bake for 30 minutes.

Tiramisu

MAKES: 8 TO 10 SERVINGS

5 eggs, separated	*1 pound ladyfingers*
½ cup sugar	*1 cup brewed espresso coffee, cooled*
½ cup Grand Marnier or	*½ cup brandy or cognac*
Frangelico liqueur	*½ cup cocoa powder*
1 pound mascarpone cheese	*½ cup confectioner's sugar*

1. Whip egg yolks, then cook them with sugar in top of a double boiler until the sugar dissolves and the mixture is smooth. Stir in liqueur and continue cooking for 10 to 20 minutes, until the mixture thickens into a custard. Remove from heat and cool.

2. In a separate bowl, whip mascarpone cheese until smooth; add to custard.

3. Beat egg whites until they form peaks; gently fold them into the custard/cheese mixture.

4. In a 9-by-13-inch baking dish or trifle bowl, make a single layer of ladyfingers.

5. Mix together coffee and brandy or cognac; drizzle half of the mixture over the ladyfingers, then spread half of the custard/cheese mixture on top.

6. Repeat steps 4 and 5, making another layer of remaining ladyfingers, coffee/liqueur, and custard.

7. Sift together cocoa and confectioner's sugar on top.

8. Refrigerate for a few hours or overnight. Slice and serve chilled.

Tip: Eggs are easier to separate when they're cold, but egg whites should be beaten at room temperature for maximum volume.

Outdoor Picnic

Along the banks of the Seine.

High in a secluded cranny of the Alps.

In your own backyard.

Wherever the spot, whatever the hour, dining alfresco can be one of life's greatest pleasures. You may want to fly a kite, play croquet, or just lie back, look up at the sky, and create cloud pictures. Any activity is sure to work up an appetite, and nothing ever tastes as good as food eaten in the fresh air. The food is simple to serve and eat, so all you'll have to do is enjoy.

Menu

Pesto Cheese Rolls

Chilled Tomato Soup

Chicken Salad with Orzo Pasta in Lettuce Cups

Iced Gingerbread

Invitations

Select cards with flowers and birds. Ask your guests to come dressed for the outdoors. (And if you'll be sitting on a blanket, tell them that, too!)

Decorations/Table Settings

- If using a picnic table, drape the table with a colorful cloth and tie up corners with ribbons. For grass seating, drape a colorful cloth over a cushiony blanket.
- For the centerpiece, tuck wildflowers or daisies into the ribbon of a large straw hat.
- Store your packed food in large baskets, or have individual baskets ready for each guest. Be sure to chill the perishable items—especially those with mayonnaise or meat—in a cooler or Thermos.

Music

Bring a portable CD player and play George Winston's *Winter into Spring* and *Linus and Lucy* albums for a light and lively touch.

Beverages

Have cold spiced iced tea or a chilled French Chablis.

Pesto Cheese Rolls

MAKES: 6 SERVINGS

8 ounces pesto
½ pound Swiss cheese, grated

1 loaf French bread, unsliced

1. In a food processor, blend together pesto and cheese until smooth.

2. Slice bread loaf in half lengthwise and scoop out the bread on both sides. Discard the soft bread. You will have two long, thin, crusty boats.

3. Fill the crusts with the cheese mixture and reassemble the loaf; wrap tightly with plastic wrap and refrigerate. To serve, slice crosswise.

Chilled Tomato Soup

MAKES: 6 SERVINGS

2 cucumbers
1 can chicken broth
Salt and pepper, to taste
2 8-ounce cans Bloody Mary mix

2 cups stewed tomatoes
2 tablespoons wine vinegar
1 cup sour cream

1. Peel and slice cucumbers, removing seeds.

2. In a small saucepan, cook cucumbers in broth for 10 to 20 minutes or until tender. Allow to cool.

3. Sprinkle with salt and pepper, to taste, and pour into a blender with Bloody Mary mix, tomatoes, and vinegar; blend well.

4. Fold in sour cream and chill.

5. Keep soup cool in Thermos until serving time.

Chicken Salad with Orzo Pasta in Lettuce Cups

MAKES: 6 SERVINGS

3 cups cooked chicken, cubed
Salt and pepper, to taste
*¼ cup oil and vinegar salad
    dressing*
1 cup mayonnaise
½ cup sour cream

1 teaspoon curry powder
1 cup celery, chopped
4 to 5 small green onions, sliced
1 cup slivered almonds
3 cups cooked orzo pasta
6 lettuce cups

1. In a large bowl, toss cooked chicken with salt, pepper, and oil and vinegar dressing.

2. In a separate bowl, mix together mayonnaise, sour cream, and curry powder; stir into chicken and blend well.

3. Add celery, onions, and almonds, then fold in pasta. Chill.

4. Spoon into lettuce cups to serve.

---

*Iced tea is so refreshing on a picnic, or anytime when you need cooling off.
For a pitcher of raspberry tea, brew 4 tea bags with ¼ cup fresh raspberries in
3 cups boiling water. Strain and mix with ¼ cup lemon juice, 1 cup sugar, and
5 cups cold water. Serve over ice.*

*Try other combinations, such as fresh ginger and mint with orange tea, or
cinnamon sticks and cloves with lemon tea. Freeze lemon slices, fresh raspberries, or mint leaves inside ice cubes, for a fun and tasty touch.*

Iced Gingerbread

MAKES: 9 SERVINGS

1 egg
½ cup sugar
½ cup oil
2 cups flour
2 teaspoons baking soda
1 teaspoon ground ginger

1 teaspoon cinnamon
½ teaspoon ground cloves
½ teaspoon salt
½ cup molasses
¾ cup boiling water

1. Preheat the oven to 350 degrees.
2. In a mixing bowl, beat together egg, sugar, and oil.
3. In a separate bowl, sift together flour and other dry ingredients.
4. Combine molasses with boiling water; mix until smooth.
5. Add the molasses mixture to the egg mixture; mix well.
6. Add the dry ingredients; mix well.
7. Pour the batter into a greased 9-by-9-inch pan.
8. Bake for 40 to 50 minutes, or until top springs back when touched. Cool and spread icing on top (icing recipe below).

Icing

1 egg white
¾ cup sugar
3 tablespoons water

2 teaspoons corn syrup
½ teaspoon cinnamon
½ teaspoon vanilla extract

1. In top of a double boiler, beat egg white with an electric mixer; gradually add sugar, water, and corn syrup.
2. Cook and beat for 3 to 4 minutes, or until the mixture is thick enough to form peaks.
3. Remove from heat and mix in cinnamon and vanilla. Spread the icing on top of the cooled gingerbread.

Romantic Dinner for Two

Your knight in shining armor.
Your princess bride.
Your spouse of twenty-five years.

Whatever the situation, hopeless romantics know nothing says romance quite as eloquently as an intimate dinner—with hearts and flowers, satin and lace, romantic music, and lots of champagne. Feed him caviar. Feed her chocolate. It's a to-die-for evening—straight from the heart.

Menu

Caviar with Toast Points

Portobello Mushroom Salad

Cornish Hens on a Bed of Wild Rice

Sautéed Green Beans

Chocolate Mousse

Invitations

Whisper in your sweetie's ear that you'd like to cook a romantic dinner—for just the two of you.

Decorations/Table Setting

- Top a small table with a white cloth and a lace runner.
- Nestle miniature ceramic cherubs or angels among sweetheart roses, and flank with candles of varying heights.
- Tie the stems of champagne glasses with white lace ribbons.
- Scatter rose petals on the table.

Music

For dinner, choose sentimental sounds from George Gershwin and Cole Porter; for really sexy moments afterward, Barry White is the best!

Beverages

Serve champagne with the caviar and a blush wine with the main course.

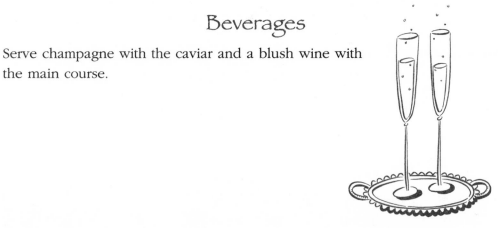

Caviar with Toast Points

MAKES: 8 TOAST POINTS

2-ounce jar caviar
1 hard-boiled egg, finely chopped

1 shallot, finely chopped
4 bread slices, toasted

1. Pile caviar in the center of a serving plate, then surround with egg and shallot bits.

2. Cut crusts off toasted bread, slice each into 4 triangles, and arrange with points up around caviar.

3. Assemble the first toast point to feed to your partner.

Portobello Mushroom Salad

MAKES: 2 SERVINGS

2 tablespoons olive oil
1 to 2 large portobello
mushrooms
1 clove garlic, minced

1 teaspoon rosemary
Boston or Bibb lettuce
Vinaigrette dressing

1. In a large skillet, warm oil over medium heat.

2. Remove and discard mushroom stems, then thinly slice the caps.

3. Sauté mushrooms and garlic for a few minutes, then sprinkle with rosemary. Cook another minute, stirring, then remove from heat and allow to cool.

4. Arrange lettuce leaves on two plates, then spoon the mushrooms on top and sprinkle lightly with vinaigrette.

Cornish Hens on a Bed of Wild Rice

MAKES: 2 SERVINGS

2 Cornish game hens, about
1½ pounds each
¼ cup olive oil
1 clove garlic, minced

¼ cup rosemary, chopped
Salt and pepper, to taste
½ cup chicken broth
2 cups cooked wild rice

1. Preheat the oven to 450 degrees.

2. Check hen cavities for giblets; remove and discard. Brush birds inside and out with olive oil, then rub with garlic and sprinkle with rosemary, salt, and pepper.

3. Place the hens into a small roasting pan and bake for 20 minutes.

4. Reduce temperature to 350 degrees and pour chicken broth over birds.

5. Cook and baste with juices about 30 minutes longer or until hens are golden brown and a leg joint is easily moved. Serve over wild rice.

Tip: Wild rice needs about 40 minutes to cook. If you put it on soon after you put the hens in the oven, the rice should be done about the same time as the hens. Check package instructions to time the cooking.

Sautéed Green Beans

MAKES: 2 SERVINGS

½ pound fresh green beans,
ends trimmed
2 tablespoons olive oil

2 tablespoons soy sauce
1 clove garlic, minced
1 teaspoon ground ginger

1. In a skillet, cook beans in hot oil over medium heat for about 5 minutes or until slightly tender.

2. Stir in remaining ingredients and simmer uncovered for a few minutes more.

Tip: Many green vegetables, such as green beans and broccoli, should be cooked uncovered, if possible; covering them will cause the color to fade.

Chocolate Mousse

MAKES: 2 SERVINGS

*2 1-ounce squares semisweet
   chocolate
2 tablespoons water*

*¼ cup confectioner's sugar
1 cup heavy cream, whipped*

1. In the top of a double boiler over simmering water, melt chocolate with 2 tablespoons water.

2. When the chocolate is smooth, use a wire whisk to add confectioner's sugar. Remove from heat and cool.

3. Fold in whipped cream, reserving 2 spoonfuls for garnish.

4. Spoon the mousse into 2 crystal bowls or brandy snifters and top with dollops of whipped cream. Chill before serving.

This romantic dinner is perfect for Valentine's Day, so use lots of red and pink, and yards of white lace:

- *Cover the table with red satin or velvet.*

- *Fill a vase with red and pink roses, accented with glittery hearts.*

- *Line the tops of dessert plates and underside of the caviar bowl with white paper doilies.*

- *Wrap candy hearts or rose petal potpourri in tulle and tie with pink bows.*

- *Use a cookie cutter to cut toasts into heart shapes.*

- *Chill the mousse in a heart-shaped mold.*

- *Serve pink champagne with raspberries in the glass. Ooh-la-la!*

Super Bowl Smash

If you can't lick 'em, join 'em. Even if you don't care for football, the best way to enjoy Super Bowl Sunday is to get into the (team) spirit of things. Decorate the TV room, serve crowd-pleasing meat and potatoes, and invite other die-hard fans to cheer on your favorite team. And it doesn't matter who wins—you'll be a smashing success!

Menu

Warm Crab Dip with Pita Chips

Green Beans and Potato Vinaigrette

Beef Tenderloin on Rolls

Caramel Brownies

Invitations

Choose football-themed cards or use the colors of your favored team. If neither of the teams is a local favorite with staunch supporters, ask your guests to dress in their college alma-mater garb.

Decorations/Table Settings

- Decorate with pennants, pom-poms, and toy footballs.
- Serve foods and beverages buffet-style, or assemble individual box lunches for guests to balance on their laps in front of the television.
- For a centerpiece, nestle a real football amidst mums festooned with flowing ribbons and miniature football figures (available at cake decorating shops).

Music

Kick things off with a collection of favorite college football songs. Have a football pool with low-dollar bets before you turn on the game.

Beverages

Serve Bloody Marys with appetizers and a merlot with dinner.

...m Crab Dip with Pita Chips

MAKES: ABOUT 3 CUPS DIP

...es cream cheese, softened
...p dry sherry
...tablespoons lemon juice
1 teaspoon curry powder

4 to 5 green onions, chopped
Salt and pepper, to taste
2 6-ounce cans crab meat, drained
Pita chips

1. Preheat the oven to 350 degrees.

2. Beat together first five ingredients, season with salt and pepper, and gently fold in crab meat.

3. Pour into crock or terrine and bake for 20 to 30 minutes or until bubbly. Serve warm with pita chips.

Green Beans and Potato Vinaigrette

MAKES: 6 SERVINGS

2 pounds new potatoes, boiled
and drained
1½ pounds fresh green beans,
boiled and drained
Salt and pepper, to taste

1 cup celery, diced
6 green onions, sliced
1 cup vinaigrette dressing
½ cup mayonnaise
½ cup sour cream

1. Toss cooked potatoes and green beans with salt and pepper.

2. Add celery and onions.

3. Pour vinaigrette dressing over all; mix well. Marinate for a few hours or overnight.

4. Drain vinaigrette marinade and toss vegetables with a mixture of mayonnaise and sour cream, adding more if desired.

Beef Tenderloin on Rolls

MAKES: 10 TO 12 SERVINGS

5 to 6 pounds beef tenderloin
4 tablespoons olive oil
1 clove garlic, minced
2 tablespoons cracked black
  pepper

1 tablespoon coarse salt
¾ cup liquid smoke
Parker House or dinner rolls
Horseradish and variety of
  mustards for condiments

1. Place beef in a large shallow pan and brush with olive oil. Mix together garlic, pepper, and salt to make a rub, then press onto the meat's surface.

2. Pour liquid smoke over all, cover, and refrigerate for a few hours or overnight.

3. Preheat the oven to 375 degrees and set for roast.

4. Remove meat from the marinade to a roasting pan and insert a meat thermometer.

5. Roast for about 40 minutes, or until thermometer reaches 140 degrees (meat will be medium-rare).

6. Remove the pan from the oven and cool the meat before slicing. Serve with sliced Parker House or dinner rolls as sandwiches, and offer condiments of horseradish and mustards.

These are not your everyday, ho-hum steak sandwiches. To accompany the tender and flavorful meat, provide a delicious, delectable, and almost-decadent selection of mustards and sauces for your beef-lovers to try. Have small dishes of Dijon with varying additions: chopped dill and chives, capers and peppercorns, garlic and onions. Offer a bowl of pungent horseradish sauce, made by mixing 3 tablespoons horseradish with 1 cup sour cream. And for the purists in the group, offer a squeeze bottle of the basic hot-dog-yellow stuff.

Caramel Brownies

MAKES: 12 BROWNIES

⅓ cup evaporated milk
50 chewy caramel candies
¾ cup butter, softened
⅓ cup milk

1 package German chocolate
cake mix
1 cup pecans, chopped
12 ounces semisweet chocolate chips

1. Preheat the oven to 350 degrees.
2. In the top of a double boiler over simmering water, stir evaporated milk with caramels until melted. Set aside.
3. Grease and flour an 8-by-12-inch baking pan.
4. Mix together butter, milk, cake mix, and pecans to form dough.
5. Press half of dough mixture into the pan. Bake for 6 minutes.
6. Remove the pan from the oven and sprinkle chocolate chips over the warm crust.
7. Dot and spread melted caramel over the chocolate. (It won't cover completely.)
8. Spread remaining dough over the caramel and return the pan to the oven for 15 to 20 minutes or until done.
9. Cool completely before cutting into bars.

Sizzling Southwest

Santa Fe.

Palm Springs.

Tucson.

Sunny days are here again—or you can pretend that they are, by treating your guests to a pueblo-inspired, desert-themed evening, complete with contemporary cuisine from the American Southwest.

Menu

Toasted Quail on Polenta Bites

Tortilla Soup

Red Snapper with Mango Salsa

Black Bean, Jicama, and Corn Salad

Marinated Papaya with Crème Fraîche

Invitations

Use desert/cactus/coyote-themed cards. Ask your guests to come dressed California-casual.

Decorations/Table Setting

- Create a patio setting with terra cotta pots of blooming cactus and whimsical coyote cutouts.
- Layer table linens in dusty desert rose and blue hues.
- Place colored votive candles in large wineglasses filled with ½ inch of water. Float small blooms around the candles.
- Fill watering cans with freshly cut sunflowers or desert roses.

Music

Fill the air with selections from contemporary artists Jim Brickman and Liz Story.

Beverages

Serve a California chardonnay.

Toasted Quail

MAKES: 6 SERVINGS

4 quail
3 tablespoons butter
1 green bell pepper, sliced

1 cup grated Monterey Jack cheese
Polenta slices

1. In a skillet, cook birds in melted butter until browned.

2. Stir in pepper slices, lower heat, cover, and cook until tender. Allow to cool, drain, and remove meat from bones.

3. Make a layer of polenta slices (recipe below) on a baking sheet, spoon quail and pepper on top, then sprinkle with cheese.

4. Place the baking sheet under a preheated broiler until the cheese melts; serve warm.

Polenta Bites

2 cups chicken broth
½ cup yellow cornmeal
¼ cup grated Parmesan cheese

1 tablespoon butter
1 tablespoon parsley, chopped

1. Preheat the oven to 375 degrees.

2. In a saucepan, bring chicken broth to a boil. Add cornmeal, reduce heat, and stir continuously for about 5 minutes, or until thick.

3. Remove from heat and fold in cheese, butter, and parsley.

4. Pour the mixture into a greased 9-by-9-inch baking pan and bake for 20 to 30 minutes or until golden. Cool slightly and slice into small squares.

You can make polenta from scratch, or purchase very good prepared polenta in 1-pound rolls in the produce or refrigerator section of your local grocery. Just slice into thin rounds and grill or spread into a pan and bake. Top with herbs and Parmesan cheese, sautéed vegetables, or your favorite salsa or pesto for a delicious side dish.

Tortilla Soup

MAKES: 6 SERVINGS

2 tablespoons oil
1 onion, chopped
2 cloves garlic, minced
*4-ounce can chopped green
    chilies*
2 cups stewed tomatoes

2 teaspoons ground cumin
Salt and pepper, to taste
6 cups chicken broth
1 cup cooked chicken, chopped
2 cups tortilla chips
Grated Monterey Jack cheese

1. Heat oil in a large pot, then add onion and garlic and sauté until tender.

2. Stir in chilies, tomatoes, cumin, salt and pepper, and broth; bring to a boil.

3. Reduce heat, add chicken pieces and tortilla chips, cover, and simmer for 20 minutes.

4. Spoon soup into bowls and top with grated cheese.

Tip: If you're lucky enough to live in an area that produces fresh tortillas, substitute 1 cup corn tortilla slices for the chips.

Red Snapper

MAKES: 6 SERVINGS

3 tablespoons olive oil
1½ pounds red snapper filets

Salt, to taste

1. Preheat the oven to 425 degrees.

2. Pour oil into a large shallow baking pan, spreading evenly. Place pan in the oven on the lower rack and heat for 5 minutes.

3. Place snapper pieces, skin side down, into the hot pan and return to oven on lower rack for about 10 minutes, or until fish is cooked. Serve skin side up, with mango salsa (recipe follows). Salt to taste.

Mango Salsa

MAKES: 6 SERVINGS

2 ripe mangoes, peeled and diced
3 tablespoons lime juice
¼ cup green onions, chopped

¼ cup cilantro, chopped
2 teaspoons chipotle peppers, minced
Salt and pepper, to taste

1. Place mango pieces into a large bowl and drizzle with lime juice.

2. Stir in remaining ingredients. Cover and chill until serving time.

Tip: Mangoes have a large seed in the center. To remove, slice and separate the fruit as you would an avocado, and scrape the fruit from the seed.

Black Bean, Jicama, and Corn Salad

MAKES: 6 SERVINGS

⅓ cup salad oil
¼ cup lime juice
3 tablespoons cilantro, chopped
½ teaspoon ground cumin
½ teaspoon salt
½ cup red onion, chopped

1 cup green pepper, chopped
2 teaspoons jalapeños, minced
1 pound jicama, peeled and chopped
2 10-ounce cans white shoepeg corn, drained
15-ounce can black beans, drained

1. In a large salad bowl, combine oil, lime juice, and spices.

2. Fold in vegetables, cover, and chill for several hours or overnight.

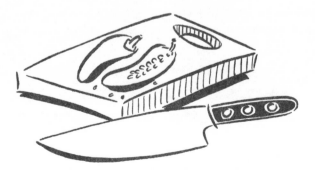

Marinated Papaya

MAKES: 6 SERVINGS

*4 to 6 ripe papayas, peeled and
    sliced*
Sugar, to taste

*¼ cup Grand Marnier or other
    fruit-flavored liqueur*

1. Divide fruit into parfait glasses or fruit cups and sprinkle lightly with sugar.

2. Pour liqueur over fruit and chill for 2 to 4 hours. (Any longer may produce
   too strong a flavor.)

3. Serve with crème fraîche topping (recipe below).

Crème Fraîche

MAKES: 2 CUPS

1 cup whipping cream

1 cup sour cream

1. Combine both creams in a mixing bowl and whip them with a wire whisk.

2. Cover the bowl and let stand at room temperature for 12 to 24 hours or
   until thick.

3. Refrigerate for another several hours until serving. Keeps in the refrigerator
   for about 2 weeks.

Taste of the Tropics

The smell of salt in the air, the sway of palm trees in the wind, and the beat of steel drums in the night.

Even if you're miles away from tropical waters, you can recreate a balmy island evening for your friends that's almost as good as the real thing.

Menu

Fried Plantains with Chutney Dip

Pineapple, Avocado, and Shrimp Salad

Jamaican Jerk Chicken

Rice and Beans with Okra

Key Lime Pie

Invitations

Roll your handwritten invitations and insert into dark long-necked bottles, then hand-deliver.

Decorations/Table Setting

- Line your front walkway or lawn with tiki torches.
- Gather potted tropical plants in your dining area.
- Spread fishnet over floral tablecloths.
- Fill dime-store fishbowls with floating tropical flowers and/or live goldfish.
- Use groupings of seashells for candleholders (secure candles with molding clay).
- Display starfish, sand dollars, and coral pieces at each place setting.

Music

Select contemporary calypso or reggae artists like Bim Sherman or Bobby McFerrin ("Don't Worry, Be Happy"). Have a bamboo stick ready in case your crowd gets into a limbo mood.

Beverages

Serve Ginger Beer or Rum Punch (see below).

Rum drinks, such as Planter's Punch, are delectable and great fun when served in a scooped-out coconut shell. For 1 serving, mix 2 jiggers rum, 2 jiggers pineapple juice, 1 jigger water, and 1 tablespoon sugar, then pour over crushed ice. Top with an orange slice and a paper umbrella, just for good measure!

Fried Plantains

MAKES: 6 SERVINGS

4 very ripe plantains   *Salt, pepper, and paprika, to taste*
Peanut oil or vegetable oil

1. Peel and remove strings from fruit. Slice very thinly and soak in a bowl of cold water 1 to 2 hours before cooking.
2. Drain and dry the plantains, then cook in a deep fryer filled with very hot oil for several minutes, or until golden brown.
3. Drain on paper towels and sprinkle with salt, pepper, and paprika.

Chutney Dip

MAKES: 1½ CUPS

6-ounce jar fruit chutney   *½ cup sour cream*
1 tablespoon lime juice

1. In a medium bowl, combine all ingredients; mix well. Chill before serving.
2. Serve as a dipping sauce for fried plantains.

Pineapple, Avocado, and Shrimp Salad

MAKES: 6 SERVINGS

6 lettuce leaves   *2 cups fresh pineapple chunks*
2 ripe avocados, peeled and sliced   *½ pound cooked baby shrimp*
1 red onion, thinly sliced   *French dressing*

1. Place lettuce leaves on individual salad plates, then layer avocados, onions, and pineapple.
2. Top with shrimp and serve with French dressing.

Jamaican Jerk Chicken

MAKES: 6 SERVINGS

1 cup soy sauce
½ cup wine vinegar
¼ cup vegetable oil
¼ cup brown sugar
¼ cup lime juice
2 Scotch bonnet or serrano chili
peppers, seeds removed

1 medium onion, chopped
2 tablespoons ground ginger
2 teaspoons ground allspice
1 teaspoon ground nutmeg
1 teaspoon ground cloves
1 teaspoon ground cinnamon
3 pounds chicken pieces, skin removed

1. Combine all ingredients except chicken in a blender or food processor and purée.
2. Place the chicken into a large bowl and pour the spice mixture on top, patting into meat; marinate for several hours or overnight.
3. Preheat the oven to 400 degrees.
4. Place the chicken into a shallow baking pan and roast for 35 to 40 minutes. Raise the baking temperature for the last few minutes to brown the chicken.

Rice and Beans with Okra

MAKES: 6 SERVINGS

1½ cups unsweetened coconut
milk
1 clove garlic, minced
4 green onions, minced
½ teaspoon thyme
1 teaspoon salt

10-ounce package frozen okra
3 cups water
14-ounce can red kidney beans,
drained
1½ cups uncooked white rice

1. In a large saucepan over medium-high heat, combine coconut milk with garlic, onions, thyme, and salt. Bring to a boil and add frozen okra.
2. Cook for a few minutes, then add water and bring to another boil. Stir in beans and rice, reduce heat, and cover.
3. Simmer for 20 minutes, then stir. Cook for an additional few minutes, or until rice is done.

Key Lime Pie

MAKES: 6 TO 8 SERVINGS

5 egg yolks
14-ounce can sweetened
  condensed milk
½ cup key lime juice

2 tablespoons lime peel, grated
9-inch graham cracker crust
Whipped cream for garnish
Lime, thinly sliced, for garnish

1. Preheat the oven to 325 degrees.

2. In a large mixing bowl, beat egg yolks at high speed for 3 to 4 minutes. Continue mixing and add condensed milk, lime juice, and lime peel, mixing well after each addition.

3. Pour the mixture into prepared crust and bake for 15 to 20 minutes or until filling is firm and set. Cool, then chill until serving time.

4. Slice the pie and garnish with whipped cream and thin lime slices.

Tip: Key lime juice has a very tart taste that gives the pie its distinctive flavor, but regular lime juice can be substituted to produce a delicious pie, too!

Flavors of Asia

Capture the ancient art of Asian cuisine with an evening reminiscent of other, more tranquil cultures. Like the spare yet sumptuous blooms you'll place in minimalist vases, this dinner is unassuming and elegant. You'll feed your senses—and your soul.

Menu

Spring Rolls with Hot Mustard

Orange/Almond Salad

Chicken Satay with Peanut Sauce

Saffron Rice

Thai Fruit Platter with Fortune Cookies

Invitations

Use rice paper and ask a calligrapher-friend to design a border of characters from any Asian language. Invite your guests to come clad in silk scarves, ties, blouses, jackets, or even pajamas!

Decorations/Table Settings

- Hang colorful paper lanterns, fans, and umbrellas.
- Layer brocade runners on tables and grace with assorted Asian porcelain and jade pieces—vases, boxes, figurines.
- Display simple blooms, such as poppies or orange blossoms, in minimalist vases.
- Use bamboo mats for table settings.
- Serve from lacquered trays and provide chopsticks as well as forks for your guests.

Music

To set the mood, try playing music by Kitaro, a popular New Age musician who fuses New Age and Asian music.

Beverages

Serve Kirin or Tsing Tao beer with appetizers and a dry white Riesling with dinner.

Spring Rolls with Hot Mustard

MAKES: 6 SERVINGS

1 pound cooked baby shrimp
1 cup cooked rice noodles,
 chopped
1 cup cabbage, minced
1 cup bean sprouts, minced
½ cup green onions, minced

Salt and pepper, to taste
12 to 16 egg roll wrappers
2 eggs, beaten
Cooking oil
Prepared hot mustard

1. In a mixing bowl, combine shrimp, noodles, and vegetables; season with salt and pepper.

2. Spread wrappers flat and spoon filling vertically down the center of each. Gently fold sides of each wrapper like an envelope and seal by brushing egg mixture along closed edges.

3. Cook in hot oil in deep fryer for about 5 minutes, or until golden brown. Serve with hot mustard sauce for dipping.

Orange/Almond Salad

MAKES: 6 SERVINGS

6 cups lettuce, shredded
2 11-ounce cans mandarin
 oranges, drained
1 cup slivered almonds
4 to 5 small green onions, chopped
1 cup salad oil

⅓ cup vinegar
⅓ cup sugar
¼ cup minced onion
1 tablespoon celery seed
1 teaspoon dry mustard
1 teaspoon salt

1. In a large salad bowl, toss together lettuce, oranges, almonds, and green onions.

2. Combine remaining ingredients and mix well to make the dressing.

3. At serving time, sparingly add the dressing to the salad, reserving extra dressing for future salads.

Chicken Satay with Peanut Sauce

MAKES: 6 SERVINGS

6 chicken breast filets	*2 teaspoons ground ginger*
½ cup soy sauce	*1 cup chunky peanut butter*
¼ cup lime juice	*½ cup cream or milk*
2 cloves garlic, minced	*4 small green onions, chopped*
2 teaspoons curry powder	*2 tablespoons lime juice*

1. Place chicken breasts in a shallow baking pan.

2. Combine soy sauce, lime juice, garlic, curry powder, and ginger; pour over chicken.

3. Cover and refrigerate for a few hours or overnight.

4. Preheat the oven to 400 degrees.

5. Remove the chicken from the refrigerator, uncover, and cook in the marinade, basting occasionally, for 45 minutes.

6. In a saucepan over low heat, stir together peanut butter, cream or milk, onions, and lime juice until blended and heated through.

7. Place chicken breasts on a serving plate or on top of saffron rice (recipe follows) and pour peanut sauce over all.

Saffron Rice

MAKES: 6 SERVINGS

½ cup green pepper, diced
4 to 5 small green onions,
  chopped
3 tablespoons butter
4 cups water

2 cups rice
1 teaspoon powdered saffron
1 teaspoon cinnamon
1 teaspoon salt
1 cup golden raisins

1. In a small skillet, sauté green pepper and onions in melted butter until cooked.

2. In a large saucepan, bring water to a boil, then add rice, spices, raisins, and sautéed vegetables. Lower heat, cover, and simmer for 20 minutes.

3. Check rice, stir, and continue cooking until rice is done and water is absorbed.

Tip: Saffron is an expensive spice, but its exquisite flavor is well worth the cost!

Thai Fruit Platter with Fortune Cookies

MAKES: 8 OR MORE SERVINGS

Lychees, whole in bunches
Mangos, peeled and sliced
Papayas, peeled and sliced

Star fruit, peeled and sliced
Kumquats
Fortune cookies

1. On lacquered or bamboo tray, arrange bunches of whole lychees (or drain from can), sliced mango, papaya, star fruit, and whole, washed kumquats.

2. Border with Chinese fortune cookies.

Tip: Kumquats are eaten whole, peel and all.

An unnervingly easy way to create a stunning dinner table is by napkin-folding. For these designs, use starched, square cloth napkins:

- Standing Fan: *Fold napkin in half to form rectangle. Starting at the short end, fold up and crease in 1-inch accordion pleats; continue about ⅔ way up. Fold in half vertically, with fan folds along the bottom. Holding with left hand, fold the right corner down to tuck into the bottom fold of pleats. Turn over and spread pleats, using tucked portion as stand to hold upright. (This is an especially beautiful accent to an Asian dinner.)*

- Standing Cone: *Fold napkin in half and roll into cone. Fold bottom point up, then fold up again to form a cuffed band. Spread bottom edges and stand on table.*

- Bishop's Hat: *Fold napkin in half diagonally, to form a triangle. Fold left and right points down to bottom point, then fold top corner down to within 1 inch of bottom corner. Fold corner back up to edge, then turn right side up and fold back sides to tuck in back. Stand and turn down two side peaks, forming a fleur-de-lis shape.*

For a buffet table, fold napkins into small envelope shapes and stack like fallen dominos, in a decorative pattern. Or insert forks and knives into the envelopes for a tucked napkin/server:

- Buffet Envelope: *Fold napkin in half, then fold top flap back one half. Turn over and fold into quarters; insert knife and fork into fold. Line up the envelopes on the buffet table next to stacked plates.*

For decorative touches, insert flower blooms, pieces of decorative raffia, or sprigs of wheat in the napkin folds or napkin rings. For a simple, yet elegant look, tie rolled napkins with ribbon or spread into a loose fan and insert into empty wineglasses at the set table.

| Standing Fan | Standing Cone | Bishop's Hat | Buffet Envelope |

Traditional Italian Feast

For centuries, Italian families have been passing down the recipe for a vegetable lasagna, improving on it all the while. Generations of Italian women—Sophia Loren, Gina Lollabrigida, even Isabella Rosellini—all swear by it. Now we've recreated it here for you. But beware: Your guests will be clamoring for the recipe. Just tell them it's an old family secret. Ciao!

Menu

Baked Garlic

Foccacia Bread with Herbed Oil

Antipasto Salad

Vegetable Lasagna

Pistachio Ice-Cream Mold

Almond Biscotti

Invitations

Use a fabric pen to handwrite your invitations on red-and-white checked bistro napkins.

Decorations/Table Setting

- Hang red, green, and white streamers with miniature Italian flags.
- Cover tables with red-and-white checked tablecloths and napkins.
- Use wax-dripped wine bottles for candlesticks.
- Create centerpieces by filling baskets with breadsticks tied with red ribbon.
- Tie a checked napkin around the wine bottle for pouring.

Music

Choose rich operatic sounds from Pavarroti or your favorite opera.

Beverages

Select a classic Italian wine, such as Chianti, Bardolino, or Valpolicella.

Baked Garlic

MAKES: 6 SERVINGS

6 large garlic heads

½ cup chicken broth

¼ cup butter, melted

Salt and pepper, to taste

1. Preheat the oven to 350 degrees.
2. Place garlic in a large shallow baking dish; pour broth and butter around the garlic.
3. Bake for 1 hour, basting 3 or 4 times.
4. Sprinkle with salt and pepper and serve warm with foccacia bread (recipe below).

Foccacia Bread

MAKES: 6 SERVINGS

10-ounce round Boboli crust

2 teaspoons olive oil

¼ cup grated Parmesan cheese

2 teaspoons rosemary, chopped

1. Preheat the oven to 450 degrees.
2. Place the crust on a baking sheet and drizzle with oil. Sprinkle Parmesan cheese and rosemary on top.
3. Bake for 8 to 10 minutes or until golden.
4. Slice the foccacia into wedges and serve with herbed oil for dipping (recipe below).

Herbed Oil

Good-quality olive oil

Garlic, minced

Basil, finely chopped

1. Pour olive oil into shallow saucer.
2. Stir in minced garlic and chopped basil.

Antipasto Salad

2 bunches romaine lettuce,
  washed and torn
12 cherry tomatoes, sliced
1 red bell pepper, sliced
1 small red onion, sliced

1 cup mushrooms, sliced
6-ounce jar artichoke hearts, drained
2-ounce can sliced black olives, drained
½ cup Italian salad dressing
¼ cup grated Parmesan cheese

1. In a large salad bowl, toss together all ingredients except dressing and cheese.
2. Add salad dressing and mix well. Sprinkle with Parmesan cheese.

Vegetable Lasagna

MAKES: 8 TO 10 SERVINGS

2 tablespoons + ¼ cup olive oil
2 cloves garlic, minced
1 cup onion, minced
1 teaspoon oregano
1 teaspoon basil, chopped
2 14-ounce cans tomato purée
1 cup zucchini, chopped
1 cup bell pepper, chopped

1 cup broccoli, chopped
1 cup mushrooms, sliced
1 cup carrots, grated
Salt and pepper, to taste
1 pound lasagna noodles
8 ounces ricotta cheese
1 pound mozzarella cheese, shredded

1. Heat 2 tablespoons olive oil in a pot over medium heat; add garlic and onion and sauté until tender. Stir in oregano, basil, and tomato purée; lower heat to simmer, stirring occasionally.
2. In a large skillet, sauté chopped vegetables in ¼ cup olive oil, stirring and cooking until tender. Season with salt and pepper.
3. Cook noodles according to package directions; drain.
4. Preheat the oven to 375 degrees.
5. In a lightly greased 9-by-13-inch baking dish, layer ⅓ of the noodles, ½ vegetables, ½ ricotta cheese, ⅓ mozzarella cheese, ⅓ tomato sauce. Repeat layers, then layer remaining noodles, tomato sauce, and mozzarella cheese.
6. Bake covered for 40 to 45 minutes; uncover for last few minutes to brown top.

Pistachio Ice-Cream Mold

MAKES: 6 TO 8 SERVINGS

1 pint pistachio ice cream
1 pint strawberry ice cream
1 pint vanilla ice cream

Candied cherries for garnish
Mint leaves for garnish

1. In a large mold, layer and freeze each flavor of ice cream, one at a time.

2. Slice and garnish with cherries and mint. Serve with almond biscotti (recipe below).

Almond Biscotti

MAKES: 3 TO 4 DOZEN

3 eggs
1½ cups sugar
¼ cup butter, softened
2¾ cups flour
1 teaspoon baking powder

½ teaspoon nutmeg
½ teaspoon salt
1 teaspoon vanilla extract
1½ cups sliced almonds

1. Preheat the oven to 350 degrees.

2. In a large mixing bowl, beat together eggs, sugar, and butter.

3. In a separate bowl, sift together flour, baking powder, nutmeg, and salt; slowly blend into the egg mixture. Fold in vanilla extract and almonds.

4. Divide mixture in half. Form each half into a 12-by-5-by-1-inch loaf. Place loves onto a greased cookie sheet. Bake for 15 to 20 minutes.

5. Remove from oven, cool loaves slightly, then cut into ½- to ¾-inch slices. Lay the slices on their sides on the cookie sheets and bake for 10 to 15 more minutes or until crisp. Cool and store in a tightly covered container.

If you want to save time, purchase ready-made biscotti, then serve with a home-made dipping sauce. Try mocha biscotti dipped in a hot fudge sauce, or lemon biscotti in a butterscotch sauce. To make a butterscotch sauce, boil together ½ cup brown sugar, ⅓ cup corn syrup, and 2 tablespoons butter, then cool and blend with ⅓ cup heavy cream. Mmm, good!

Mexican Fiesta

It's fiesta time, with inspiration from our friends south of the border, down Mexico way. Details, details. It's all in the details: serapes, piñatas, and the intensity of the flavors and aromas of peppers—some hot, and some not. This dinner party is so easy—and your guests will think you've been laboring intensely in the kitchen for days. You'll love it, and they will, too. Olé!

Menu

Stuffed Jalapeños

Mexican Salsa (with tortilla chips)

Chili con Queso Dip (with blue corn chips
or white tortilla chips)

Guacamole Salad

Make-Your-Own Tostadas

Flan

Invitations

Use cards bordered with chili peppers or Mexican sombreros. Ask your guests to come dressed in colorful embroidered cottons.

Decorations/Table Setting

- Set the mood with luminarias to light up your sidewalk or patio. To make them yourself, weigh down brightly colored sacks with sand and place votive candles in glass votive cups on the bottoms. Light at dusk.
- Drape tables with striped serapes or brightly colored cloths.
- Fill pottery pieces with paper flowers and bunches of dried peppers for a centerpiece.
- Serve chips in a large straw sombrero, which can be used later for an impromptu hat dance.
- Hang a piñata filled with candies. After dinner, let blindfolded guests take turns swinging at the piñata!

Music

Play a contemporary CD from The Gypsy Kings or use a traditional collection of mariachi songs, such as "Guadalajara" and "La Cucaracha."

Beverages

Serve Mexican beer, such as Corona or Dos Equis, and toast with the words, *"Salud, dinero, y amor."* (Health, wealth, and love.) Or whip up margaritas in the blender (see sidebar, page 94).

Stuffed Jalapeños

MAKES: 6 SERVINGS (2 JALAPEÑOS PER SERVING)

12 large pickled jalapeño
*   peppers*
1 cup whipped cream cheese
3 to 4 green onions, minced

½ cup grated cheddar or
*   Monterey Jack cheese*
¼ cup cilantro, chopped
3-ounce jar pimiento slices

1. Preheat the oven to 375 degrees.

2. Slice a pocket in each pepper lengthwise, leaving stem attached. Carefully scoop out seeds and interior membranes.

3. Mix together cheese with onion and spoon into pepper shells.

4. Place the stuffed peppers on a greased cookie sheet and sprinkle with cilantro and pimiento slices. Bake for 8 to 10 minutes or until bubbly.

Tip: Jalapeños are not for the faint of heart! Wear rubber gloves when preparing and have water nearby when eating. And *never* touch your eyes after handling raw jalapeños!

Mexican Salsa

MAKES: 2 CUPS

3 ripe tomatoes, finely chopped
1 small onion, finely chopped
⅓ cup jalapeño peppers, finely
*   chopped*

2 tablespoons cilantro, chopped
1 tablespoon lemon juice
Salt, to taste

1. Mix together all ingredients and refrigerate.

2. Serve cool or at room temperature with tortilla chips.

Tip: For a more flavorful salsa, allow it to stand a few days before serving.

Chili con Queso Dip

MAKES 5 CUPS

16-ounce can chopped tomatoes

3-ounce can chopped green chilies

2-pound package Velveeta cheese, cubed

Blue corn chips or white tortilla chips

1. In a double boiler over simmering water, or in a microwave, heat together all ingredients until the cheese melts. Stir and blend until smooth.

2. Serve warm with blue corn chips or white tortilla chips.

Guacamole Salad

MAKES: 6 SERVINGS

3 ripe avocados

2 tablespoons lime juice

Garlic salt, to taste

1 ripe tomato, finely chopped

1 small onion, finely chopped

3 tablespoons salsa

2 tablespoons mayonnaise

1 teaspoon chili powder

1. Slice avocados in half, reserving seeds. Scoop out pulp, mash with a fork, and sprinkle with lime juice and garlic salt.

2. Fold in remaining ingredients and serve immediately.

Tip: If not serving guacamole immediately, press avocado seeds back into the mixture, cover with plastic wrap, and refrigerate. Seeds will help preserve color and freshness for another 2 to 3 hours.

Toast your guests with a margarita, the drink of choice south of the border. Coat the rims of 4 large wineglasses with lemon juice, then dip the rims into a saucer of salt. In a blender, mix 2 cups ice chips, 1¼ cups tequila, a 6-ounce can of thawed frozen limeade concentrate, and ⅓ cup triple sec or Cointreau liqueur. Blend on high until slushy and pour into prepared glasses. Muy delicioso!

Make-Your-Own Tostadas

MAKES: 12 SERVINGS

3 pounds boneless pork roast
1 pound dried pinto beans,
  presoaked in water
7 cups water
2 onions, chopped
2 tablespoons chili powder
1 tablespoon ground cumin

1 teaspoon garlic, minced
2 dozen fried flat corn tortillas
2 heads lettuce, shredded
3 tomatoes, chopped
3 cups grated Cheddar cheese
2 cups sour cream

1. Place roast, beans, water, onions, and spices in a large roasting pan or crock pot. Cook covered on low for 5 to 6 hours or until meat is done.

2. With a fork, shred the tender meat and mix it with the beans.

3. Serve on top of crispy tortillas and offer lettuce, tomato, cheese, and sour cream as garnishes.

Flan

MAKES: 6 TO 8 SERVINGS

½ cup brown sugar
6 eggs
¾ cup sugar

2 14-ounce cans evaporated milk
2 teaspoons vanilla

1. Preheat the oven to 350 degrees.

2. Spread brown sugar on the bottom of an 8-inch round baking dish or cake pan and place in the oven for 30 minutes.

3. In a mixing bowl, beat eggs, gradually adding sugar, evaporated milk, and vanilla. Continue beating for 1 minute or until the sugar dissolves.

4. Pour custard mix over the brown sugar and place the 8-inch dish into a larger shallow pan; pour hot water around the dish.

5. Bake for 1 hour, or until knife inserted into the center comes out clean. Cool and refrigerate.

6. To serve, run a knife along the edge of the chilled pan, invert the flan onto a serving plate, and slice into wedges.

Middle Eastern Elegance

Like a magic carpet ride or a trip through a colorful, exotic bazaar, such is the sense of delight you create with the profusion of exquisite spices and easy elegance native to this culture.

Menu

Hummus Dip with Pita Chips

Feta Cheese and Tomato Salad

Lamb Kebabs

Couscous with Eggplant

Baklava

Invitations

Select cards with ornate batik and gold borders; write with gold metallic ink.

Decorations/Table Setting

- Set the mood with aromatic incense and groupings of lush, green potted plants.
- Hang heavy tapestries and batik.
- Layer lush, rich cloths with exotic runners and trim with gold cord and tassels.
- Cluster ornate copper, pewter, and brass jars and vases to hold candles and peacock feathers for the centerpieces.

Music

Play the soundtrack from *Zorba the Greek*. Warning: The music may inspire belly-dancing among the guests! (To encourage that sort of behavior, hire a dancer to demonstrate some basic moves.)

Beverages

Serve a hearty red wine with dinner; after dinner, treat your guests to the Greek liqueur ouzo on ice. (Ouzo tastes strongly like black licorice.)

Hummus Dip with Pita Chips

MAKES: 6 SERVINGS

1-pound can garbanzo beans,
  drained
⅓ cup lemon juice
3 tablespoons sesame seed paste
  (tahini)
3 tablespoons parsley, chopped

1 garlic clove, minced
Salt, to taste
Artichoke, hollowed out
2-ounce jar sliced pimientos
Pita chips

1. In a food processor, blend together garbanzo beans, lemon juice, tahini, parsley, and garlic.

2. Add salt to taste and spoon into a hollowed-out artichoke.

3. Garnish with pimientos. Serve with pita chips.

We've suggested serving the hummus dip in a hollowed-out artichoke, but many other vegetables can be called into service to hold dips, salads, and sauces, as well. Try acorn squash and eggplant with decoratively trimmed edges, or the always-beautiful tomato "rose": Make 6 to 8 slices down a tomato, almost to the bottom. Then use a small, sharp knife to peel the top outer skin down and away, forming curls. Fill with spreads, dips, and so on, and surround with colorful cabbage leaves or bright radishes.

Feta Cheese and Tomato Salad

MAKES: 6 SERVINGS

6 ripe tomatoes, chopped
½ pound feta cheese, crumbled
1 cup black olives, sliced

Vinaigrette dressing
Lettuce leaves

1. Combine tomatoes with cheese and olives in a salad bowl.

2. Toss with vinaigrette and serve on lettuce leaves.

Lamb Kebabs

MAKES: 6 SERVINGS

½ cup olive oil
⅓ cup dry sherry
3 cloves garlic, minced
2 teaspoons oregano
1 teaspoon salt
½ teaspoon pepper

3 pounds lamb, cut in bite-size
  pieces
3 green peppers, cut in bite-size
  pieces
3 zucchini, cut in bite-size pieces
12 cherry tomatoes
12 white onion pieces

1. Combine oil, sherry, and spices in a shallow dish; place lamb pieces into the marinade, cover, and refrigerate for a few hours or overnight.

2. Skewer lamb and vegetable pieces, alternating each, on six skewers; baste with remaining marinade.

3. Cook under a preheated broiler for 5 to 6 minutes on each side, or until done.

Couscous with Eggplant

MAKES: 6 SERVINGS

½ cup butter
1 onion, chopped
1 eggplant, peeled and chopped
3 cups chicken broth
¼ cup lemon juice

½ cup basil, chopped
1 teaspoon ground ginger
Salt, to taste
1½ cups couscous

1. Heat butter in a large pot over medium heat, add onion and eggplant, and sauté for about 20 minutes, or until tender.

2. Add chicken broth, lemon juice, basil, ginger, and salt; bring to a boil.

3. Stir in couscous, cover, and turn off heat. Let stand for about 10 minutes, or until liquid is absorbed and couscous is fluffy.

Baklava

MAKES: 6 SERVINGS

1 pound frozen phyllo dough,
thawed
½ pound butter, melted
1 pound crushed walnuts
¾ cup sugar

3 teaspoons cinnamon
½ cup honey
¼ cup sugar
¼ cup water
1 tablespoon lemon juice

1. Preheat the oven to 400 degrees.

2. Place 1 sheet of dough on a large ungreased baking sheet and brush with melted butter. Continue to layer sheets with butter until ½ of dough is used.

3. Combine crushed nuts with ¾ cup sugar and cinnamon and spread evenly over top of dough. Place another sheet of dough over nut mixture, brush with butter, and continue layering phyllo sheets.

4. Slice into 2-by-2-inch squares or 3-inch rectangles. Bake for about 15 minutes until golden. Cool.

5. In a small saucepan, combine honey, ¼ cup sugar, water, and lemon juice and bring to a boil; cook for a few minutes until the sugar dissolves and the mixture is well blended. Cool and pour over baklava to glaze.

Tip: If this sounds like a lot of work—it is! Of course, you can put in the effort and take the well-deserved praise. If time is limited, however, remember that most bakeries and gourmet shops carry very good prepared baklava.

New Orleans Celebration

If you ever need an excuse for a party, celebrate the king of all parties—Mardi Gras! The glitter of festival beads, the delights of shrimp and crab, and the tastes of the Creole cuisine. . . . Delicious? Yes. Decadent? You bet. Sure to make you a star? Absolutely.

Menu

Crab Cakes with Remoulade Dipping Sauce

Caesar Salad with French Bread

Shrimp Creole on Rice Beds

Bread Pudding with Bourbon Sauce

Invitations

Make colorful purple Mardi Gras masks with feathers and glitter. Write in gold metallic ink.

Decorations/Table Setting

- Decorate with fern branches and bougainvillea blooms to recreate the French Quarter.
- Use green and purple—the colors of the festival—in table coverings and glittery banners.
- Group sparkler candles in shiny holders.
- Arrange ornate party masks, ostrich feathers, and ferns in a vase as the centerpiece.
- Place party horns and confetti next to each place setting. (You can clean up the mess later—as Scarlett O'Hara said, "Tomorrow's another day.")

Music

Play your favorite jazz or anything from Harry Connick, Jr. "When the Saints Go Marching In" from Louis Armstrong is a must.

Beverages

Serve gin fizzes or rum punch with appetizers, and a white Burgundy with dinner.

Crab Cakes

1 pound crabmeat
2 cups bread crumbs
⅓ cup onion, minced
2 tablespoons parsley, chopped

1 egg
2 tablespoons water
Vegetable oil

1. In a mixing bowl, combine crabmeat with bread crumbs, onion, and parsley; mix well.
2. In a separate bowl, beat egg and water with a fork until frothy.
3. Fold the egg mixture into the crab mixture; mix well.
4. Form the mixture into small patties.
5. Heat oil in a large skillet and sauté crab cakes for several minutes on each side, or until golden brown.
6. Serve with remoulade sauce for dipping (recipe below).

Remoulade Dipping Sauce

1 cup mayonnaise
2 tablespoons Dijon mustard
¼ cup salad oil
1 tablespoon vinegar

1 tablespoon horseradish
1 tablespoon onion, minced
1 tablespoon parsley, chopped
1 teaspoon paprika

1. Combine all ingredients and blend well.
2. Chill until serving.
3. Serve with warm crab cakes.

Caesar Salad with French Bread

MAKES: 6 SERVINGS

½ cup olive oil

2 teaspoons wine vinegar

2 teaspoons prepared Dijon
  mustard

1 tablespoon lemon juice

1 tablespoon anchovy paste

1 clove garlic, minced

1 teaspoon pepper

2 heads romaine lettuce

2 cups garlic croutons

½ cup grated Parmesan cheese

Sliced French bread

1. Combine oil, vinegar, mustard, lemon juice, anchovy paste, garlic, and pepper; blend thoroughly.

2. Place washed and torn lettuce leaves in a large salad bowl. Add enough dressing to coat, then toss in croutons and Parmesan cheese.

3. Serve with crusty French bread.

Tip: If you use the anchovy paste in this recipe (or any others), test before seasoning with extra salt. Anchovies can be very salty. Anchovy paste is available in tubes, which are very convenient and practical.

———————————————————

Nothing goes better with fresh, crusty bread than cold, sweet cream butter. And when company is coming, why not dress up the butter for the occasion? Try these ideas:

- *Thinly slice a stick of butter and arrange the slices in an overlapping pattern. Garnish with a sprig of parsley.*

- *Press soft butter into lined decorative candy molds. Chill and turn out onto a doily-lined plate.*

- *Use a melon-baller to scoop out butter balls. Chill and stack in a pretty dish.*

- *Spread softened butter into egg cups. Draw designs on top with fork tines.*

- *Heat a butter curler in hot water and draw across surface of a butter stick. Drop curls into cold water and chill. Drain before serving.*

Shrimp Creole on Rice Beds

MAKES: 6 SERVINGS

3 tablespoons butter	*1 tablespoon Worcestershire sauce*
1 cup onion, chopped	*2 drops Tabasco*
1 cup celery, chopped	*½ cup water*
1 tablespoon flour	*2 pounds cleaned raw shrimp*
½ teaspoon salt	*1 teaspoon cornstarch*
½ teaspoon pepper	*Cooked white rice*
10-ounce can stewed tomatoes	

1. Heat butter in a large saucepan, add onion and celery, and sauté until tender.

2. Sprinkle flour, salt, and pepper over vegetables, then stir in tomatoes, Worcestershire sauce, and Tabasco.

3. Add water and bring to a boil.

4. Reduce heat, stir in shrimp, and simmer for 15 to 20 minutes, adding more water if needed.

5. Stir in cornstarch to thicken.

6. Serve over hot white rice.

Tip: When adding cornstarch, I recommend pouring a few tablespoons of the liquid you are trying to thicken into a separate bowl, then adding cornstarch and blending well. Add the resulting mixture to your dish and mix to distribute evenly. This way you are less likely to have lumps of cornstarch in your food.

Bread Pudding

MAKES: 6 SERVINGS

1 loaf French bread, cubed
4 tablespoons butter, melted
3 cups milk
4 eggs, beaten
½ cup sugar

1 tablespoon vanilla
1 teaspoon cinnamon
½ teaspoon nutmeg
Whipped cream for garnish (optional)

1. Preheat the oven to 375 degrees.

2. Place bread into a greased 9-inch baking dish and drizzle with melted butter.

3. In a separate saucepan, scald milk and stir in eggs, sugar, vanilla, and spices. Pour over the bread, stirring to moisten.

4. Bake for 30 minutes. Serve warm with whipped cream or bourbon sauce (recipe below).

Bourbon Sauce

MAKES: 3 CUPS

2 cups vanilla ice cream
½ cup milk

½ cup bourbon

1. Combine all ingredients in a blender and blend until smooth.

2. Serve immediately over warm bread pudding.

Simple Pleasures of Provence

Ahh . . . the joys of Provence! The mingling of sights, sounds, and scents as you stroll through markets full of fragrant flowers and fresh fish caught in local waters; as you hike through hills lush with aromatic herbs, surrounded by the enticing aroma of lavender and rosemary; or as you relax on a sunny terrace, sipping a glass of very good local wine. Recreate the romance of this most marvelous of French experiences—one that is exceedingly simple, yet extravagantly satisfying.

Menu

Chicken Liver Pâté with French Bread

Ratatouille Salad

Swordfish with Herbes de Provence Sauce

Roasted Potatoes

Blueberry Clafoutis

Invitations

Use picture postcards from Provence (the French southeastern coast) or write your message on informal notes with pretty Country French prints on the front.

Decorations/Table Settings

Transform your patio or dining room into a Riviera cafe:
- Drape tables with Provence linen cloths or runners.
- Group pots of fragrant herbs and bright geraniums for color and scent, and have small herb topiaries for centerpieces.
- Wrap votive candles with waxy green leaves and tie with colorful yarn.
- Sprinkle green leaves on the tabletop.
- Write the menu in French on a chalkboard easel.

Music

Try to find the CD *Provence* from the record label Ocora. This collection of a variety of artists is widely available.

Beverages

Choose a white Bordeaux, or select several varieties for a wine-tasting (see below).

Select an array of wines for an informal wine-tasting. Arrange bottles on a table with place cards identifying each—include the name, vineyard, country, and year. Have plenty of inexpensive wineglasses available. Enjoy!

Chicken Liver Pâté with French Bread

MAKES: 6 SERVINGS

2 tablespoons butter	*1 teaspoon ground cloves*
2 tablespoons olive oil	*½ teaspoon nutmeg*
1 onion, minced	*¼ cup dry sherry*
1 pound chicken livers, chopped	*¼ cup cream*
Salt and pepper, to taste	*French bread slices*

1. In a large skillet over medium heat, melt butter with olive oil; add onions and sauté until tender.

2. Stir in livers and season with salt and pepper. Add cloves and nutmeg and continue cooking until liver is brown on the outside.

3. Remove from heat, stir in sherry and allow to cool.

4. Place the mixture in a blender or food processor and add cream. Process until smooth.

5. Transfer to a crock or terrine and chill until serving. Serve as spread with French bread slices.

Ratatouille Salad

MAKES: 6 SERVINGS

½ cup olive oil	*2 zucchini, sliced*
1 onion, chopped	*3 large tomatoes, chopped*
1 clove garlic, minced	*Salt and pepper, to taste*
2 eggplants, chopped	*2 teaspoons basil, chopped*
2 green peppers, chopped	

1. Heat olive oil in a large skillet; add onion and garlic and sauté until the onion is tender.

2. Stir in remaining ingredients, lower the heat, and simmer covered for about 30 minutes or until vegetables are tender.

3. Remove from heat and allow to cool. Drain and refrigerate until serving.

Tip: For this recipe, and others, peel eggplant last—just before using. The eggplant flesh will discolor quickly.

Swordfish

MAKES: 6 SERVINGS

6 swordfish steaks, about
½ pound each

1 cup dry white wine
Salt, to taste

1. Preheat the oven to 375 degrees.

2. Place fish in a large shallow baking dish in a single layer.

3. Pour wine over the fish and sprinkle with salt.

4. Bake for about 10 minutes (turning once). Fish flakes when done. Serve with Herbes de Provence Sauce (recipe below).

Herbes de Provence Sauce

MAKES: 6 SERVINGS

⅓ cup olive oil
1 onion, chopped
2 cloves garlic, minced
6 ripe tomatoes, finely chopped
2 cups dry red wine
1 cup water

2 tablespoons parsley, chopped
2 tablespoons thyme, chopped
2 tablespoons marjoram, chopped
1 cup black olives, sliced
¼ cup capers

1. Heat olive oil in a large skillet; add onions and garlic and sauté until the onions are tender. Add tomatoes, wine, water, parsley, thyme, and marjoram.

2. Reduce heat, cover, and simmer, stirring regularly and adding more water if necessary. Cook until tomatoes are soft, about 30 minutes.

3. Remove from heat, stir in olives and capers, and spoon over cooked swordfish.

Tip: Since capers usually come packed in a salt or brine liquid, you may choose to drain and rinse them before adding to recipes.

Roasted Potatoes

MAKES: 6 SERVINGS

6 large potatoes
Cold water
½ cup butter, melted

1 clove garlic, minced
Paprika, salt, and pepper, to taste

1. Preheat the oven to 450 degrees.
2. Wash potatoes but do not peel. Slice into long strips and place in cold water for 10 minutes. Then drain, dry, and place in a large shallow baking pan.
3. Drizzle with melted butter and garlic; stir to coat.
4. Bake uncovered for 35 to 40 minutes, turning at least once.
5. Season with paprika, salt, and pepper. Serve warm.

Blueberry Clafoutis

MAKES: 6 SERVINGS

2 cups fresh blueberries
¼ cup + ¼ cup granulated
* sugar*
2 eggs
1½ cups milk
1 tablespoon butter, melted

⅓ heaping cup flour
¼ teaspoon salt
½ teaspoon vanilla
¼ cup confectioner's sugar
Blueberries for garnish
Fresh mint leaves for garnish

1. Preheat the oven to 400 degrees.
2. Sprinkle blueberries with ¼ cup sugar and stir to coat. Spread the berries in the bottom of a greased 8-inch round tart pan.
3. Stir together eggs, milk, melted butter, flour, salt, and remaining ¼ cup sugar; blend until smooth.
4. Add vanilla and mix well.
5. Pour the batter over the blueberries.
6. Bake for 20 minutes, then reduce heat to 325 degrees and continue baking for 10 to 15 minutes more, or until golden and puffed.
7. Sift confectioner's sugar on top of the warm pastry and let cool before serving.
8. Garnish with fresh blueberries and mint leaves.

Russian Repast

For centuries, we've been fascinated with the extravagant and dramatic lives of the Russian czars. Let our *Dr. Zhivago* theme recreate the glamour and allure of that elegant era. This is the dinner Julie Christie would have served to Omar Sharif. *Na zdorovye!* ("To your health"—the Russian version of "Cheers!")

Menu

Caviar Mold with Crackers

Borscht (with Bakery Rye Bread)

Chicken Kiev

Boiled Potatoes with Dill

Stewed Red Cabbage

Charlotte Russe

Invitations

Tie invitations to miniature vodka bottles, and invite your guests to dine like the Russian czars. Hand-deliver in padded envelopes.

Decorations/Table Setting

- Hang travel posters depicting Russian themes, or enlarge old Absolut ads.
- Display Russian-style fur hats with red streamers.
- Cover tables with maps of the former USSR, and place toy trains in the center, festooned with small red flowers as cargo.
- If possible, use large brightly colored Russian shawls to cover tables and/or chair backs, or simply strew them about to create a warm and inviting setting.
- If you can lay your hands on one, display a samovar on or near the dinner table. If you have one that works, add a wonderful touch of authenticity to your dinner by using the samovar to make and serve tea after dinner.
- Decorate the table and the room with matryoshkas (wooden nesting dolls), wooden spoons, or other colorful wooden folk art items.

Music

Play the soundtrack from *Dr. Zhivago,* and rent the movie to play in the background, adding to the mood. If you can find any authentic Russian music, all the better—old Russian songs can be very soulful, and many are performed by guitars, balalaikas, and other stringed instruments.

Beverages

Serve small glasses of chilled vodka straight up with the caviar, and a hearty white Moselle wine with dinner.

Caviar Mold with Crackers

MAKES: 6 TO 8 SERVINGS

8 ounces whipped cream cheese,
   softened
2 tablespoons sour cream
1 tablespoon mayonnaise

1 tablespoon lemon juice
½ teaspoon Worcestershire sauce
6 ounces caviar
Crackers

1. Mix all ingredients, except caviar and crackers, in a blender until smooth; turn out onto a serving plate and form into a dome.

2. Cover the top with caviar and surround with crackers.

Caviar never goes out of style. And although it carries grand connotations, it doesn't have to be a budget-breaker. The most expensive is beluga, but other less costly grades are delicious, too, such as the osetra or sevruga varieties. Caviar is easy to serve—just spoon into a bowl embedded in crushed ice, and spread onto toast. Or create an elegant presentation with garnishes of sour cream, minced onion, and diced hard-cooked egg, garnished with sprigs of parsley, and surrounded by crackers for spreading. You'll see why it's called the "food of the gods."

Borscht

MAKES: 6 SERVINGS

¼ cup butter
2 cups white cabbage, chopped
1 cup carrots, shredded
1 cup onion, chopped
3 cans condensed beef broth
4 cups water
2 cups canned beets, diced

2 tablespoons parsley, chopped
1 bay leaf
2 cloves garlic, minced
1 cup potato, diced
Salt and pepper, to taste
1 cup sour cream
Bakery rye bread

1. Heat butter in a large saucepan, then add cabbage, carrots, and onion and sauté for about 5 minutes. Add beef broth and water and bring to boil.

2. Add beets, parsley, bay leaf, and garlic. Reduce heat; simmer for 30 minutes.

3. Add potatoes, salt, and pepper and continue cooking for 30 more minutes. Remove bay leaf.

4. Spoon borscht into serving bowls and top with a dollop of sour cream. Serve with rye bread on the side.

Tip: Borscht tastes better the next day, so prepare it a day ahead, then reheat.

Chicken Kiev

MAKES: 8 SERVINGS

8 chicken breast halves, deboned
* and skinned*
1 clove garlic, minced
2 tablespoons parsley, chopped
2 tablespoons chives, minced

Salt and pepper, to taste
1 stick butter
2 eggs, beaten
2 cups bread crumbs
Cooking oil

1. Pound breast halves until they are thin and lay flat.

2. Combine garlic, parsley, and chives and spread onto each chicken piece.

3. Season with salt and pepper and place 1 tablespoon butter in the center of each breast half. Roll chicken to enclose butter and secure with a toothpick.

4. Coat each roll with beaten egg, then with bread crumbs.

5. Cook in hot oil in a deep fryer until the crust is golden and the chicken is cooked through, about 6 minutes. Remove toothpicks before serving.

Boiled Potatoes with Dill

MAKES: 6 SERVINGS

*3 pounds potatoes, peeled and
  chopped*
Salt and pepper, to taste

1 stick butter
1 clove garlic, minced
½ cup fresh dill, chopped

1. In a large saucepan, place potatoes into boiling water, cover, lower heat, and simmer for 45 minutes, or until tender. Drain and season with salt and pepper.

2. Melt butter with garlic in the microwave and stir in dill. Toss with potatoes to coat.

Stewed Red Cabbage

MAKES: 6 SERVINGS

¼ cup butter
4 cups red cabbage, shredded
½ cup onion, chopped
1 clove garlic, minced

½ cup water
½ cup tomato paste
Salt and pepper, to taste

1. Heat butter in a large pot, then add cabbage, onion, and garlic and sauté for 5 to 10 minutes.

2. Stir together water and tomato paste and add to the cabbage. Bring to a boil, then lower heat to simmer, cover, and cook for 30 minutes, stirring occasionally and adding more water if necessary. When cabbage is tender, season with salt and pepper.

Tip: Keep an eye on the cabbage to see if it needs more water. The cabbage should give off a fair amount of water on its own, and this dish should sauté, not boil. However, it shouldn't burn, either.

Charlotte Russe

MAKES: 6 SERVINGS

¼-ounce envelope unflavored
  gelatin
½ cup sugar
2 cups milk
4 egg yolks
1 teaspoon vanilla extract

4 egg whites
1 dozen large ladyfingers, split or
  sliced
Berries for garnish
Whipped cream for garnish

1. In a small saucepan, combine gelatin, sugar, and milk and cook over medium heat just until milk begins to boil.

2. Remove from heat and stir in egg yolks, then return to medium heat, cooking and stirring constantly for about 5 minutes or until thickened.

3. Stir in vanilla and allow custard to cool to room temperature (about 30 minutes), then refrigerate.

4. In a large bowl, beat egg whites with an electric mixer until they form stiff peaks. Fold into cooled custard.

5. Lightly grease a dessert mold or springform pan and line the bottom with wax paper. Place split ladyfingers vertically, curved side out, along sides of the mold.

6. Carefully spoon filling into the mold and refrigerate until firm, several hours or overnight.

7. Loosen around edges with a knife and turn out onto a serving plate. Garnish with berries and whipped cream before slicing.

Swiss Fondue

Do you long to be schussing in St. Moritz? Hobnobbing in Gstaad? Create a cozy Swiss fondue party that's swanky, but not stuffy—maybe you'll even sit on the floor! At any rate, this dinner theme provides one of the most convivial settings possible for a dinner party as guests spear, swirl, and savor together in an informal and very cozy setting. Let candlelight cast a glow, let your guests partake of sumptuous dipping sauces, and let yourself bathe in the accolades that are sure to come at evening's end.

Menu

Mulled Wine

Hot Buttered Rum

Roasted Pepper Canapés

Cheese Fondue with French Bread

Mixed Green Salad with Vinaigrette

Beef Bourguignonne Fondue with
Horseradish Sauce

Chocolate Fondue with Strawberries
and Angel Food Cake

Invitations

Use preprinted Alpine-themed invitations, or paint the Swiss flag in the corner of a card. Ask your guests to "think snow" in their dress.

Decorations/Table Setting

Create a Swiss chalet atmosphere:

- Cover walls with ski posters.
- Stack your old skiing equipment in the doorway.
- Hang wool caps and mittens from the chandelier.
- Cover the floor with a bearskin rug (in front of the fireplace, if possible).
- For the adventurous, arrange low tables with floor cushions for a casual and fun seating arrangement. (Whether you use floor seating or a traditional dining table, suitably cover the tables for the dripping that's sure to occur.)
- Make fondue pots the focal point of your table.
- Arrange pine cones and fragrant evergreen branches on the tables. Insert large candles into jugs and nestle the jugs among the branches. (Take care to place the branches safely away from the canned heat or alcohol flames.)

Music

Alternate Strauss with selections from Sigmund Romberg's *The Student Prince*. (And if your guests start yodeling, that's okay, too!)

Beverages

Have hot buttered rum or mulled wine ready as the party begins (see recipes), and serve an Alsatian wine—perhaps Moselle—with dinner.

Mulled Wine

1 quart red Burgundy wine
3 ripe oranges, sliced
3 ripe lemons, sliced
1 cup sugar

4 cinnamon sticks, broken
¼ cup whole cloves
Cinnamon sticks for garnish

1. In a large saucepan, combine all ingredients except garnish. Bring just to boiling over medium to high heat, stirring until the sugar dissolves.

2. Reduce heat and simmer for at least 10 minutes.

3. Strain to remove fruit and cloves and pour into mugs.

4. Garnish with cinnamon sticks and serve warm.

Hot Buttered Rum

1 stick butter, softened
1 pound brown sugar
½ teaspoon ground cinnamon

¼ teaspoon ground cloves
Dark rum
Boiling water

1. Cream together butter, brown sugar, and spices. Refrigerate until ready to serve. (This batter can be prepared the day before.)

2. For each serving, spoon a heaping tablespoon of butter batter into a mug and add 1½ ounces rum.

3. Fill to the top with boiling water and stir.

Roasted Pepper Canapés

MAKES: 8 TO 10 SERVINGS

6 large red and green bell peppers
¼ cup olive oil
¼ cup lemon juice
2 cloves garlic, minced

1 teaspoon oregano
1 teaspoon basil
½ teaspoon salt
Large crackers or toasts

1. Place peppers under a preheated broiler for about 5 minutes on each side, or until skin completely browns.

2. Remove peppers from the oven and let cool for a few minutes; then cut out stems and seeds and peel off outer skin. Cut into slivers ½ inch wide and arrange in a shallow dish.

3. Combine remaining ingredients and pour over peppers; allow to marinate several hours before serving.

4. Drain and spoon the peppers onto large crackers or toasts.

Cheese Fondue with French Bread

MAKES: 8 SERVINGS

2 cups dry white wine
1 teaspoon lemon juice
2 pounds grated Gruyere cheese
¼ cup kirsch (a strong cherry-
   flavored liqueur)

1 tablespoon cornstarch
Dash of nutmeg
French bread, cubed

1. Cook wine and lemon juice in a fondue pot until very hot. Decrease heat and stir in cheese, cooking until melted.

2. In a separate bowl, blend kirsch with cornstarch and nutmeg; stir into cheese until smooth. Keep on low heat and do not boil.

3. Serve as a dip for French bread.

Mixed Green Salad with Vinaigrette

MAKES: 8 SERVINGS

1 head red leaf lettuce
1 head green leaf lettuce
1 head romaine lettuce
1 cup bell pepper, chopped
1 cup mushrooms, sliced
4 to 6 cherry tomatoes, sliced

3 tablespoons red wine vinegar
2 tablespoons Dijon mustard
1 teaspoon sugar
½ teaspoon salt
¾ cup oil

1. Wash greens and tear into bite-size pieces. Combine with pepper, mushrooms, and tomatoes in a large salad bowl.

2. In a small separate dish, mix together vinegar, mustard, sugar, salt, and oil. Toss with salad just before serving.

Beef Bourguignonne Fondue with Horseradish Sauce

MAKES: 8 TO 10 SERVINGS

Ingredients for Sauce:
1 cup sour cream
⅓ cup prepared horseradish

½ teaspoon lemon juice

Ingredients for Beef:
2 cups peanut oil
½ pound butter

4 pounds beef sirloin or tenderloin,
cut into ¾-inch cubes

1. Mix together sour cream, horseradish, and lemon juice. Chill until serving time.

2. Heat oil and butter together in a fondue pot and allow guests to cook meat to their own preference: 20 seconds for rare and about 1 minute for well done.

3. Serve with sauce for dipping.

Chocolate Fondue with Strawberries and Angel Food Cake

MAKES: 8 SERVINGS

24 ounces semisweet chocolate
  chips
¼ cup water
½ cup heavy cream

¼ cup brandy or liqueur
1 quart fresh strawberries, washed,
  stems removed
1 platter angel food cake cubes

1. Melt chocolate chips with water in a microwave. Stir in cream and brandy, blending until smooth.

2. Place the mixture into a fondue pot over a warmer and serve as dip for strawberries and cake pieces.

"Fondue" comes from the French word for melting and blending, and enjoys a fine history on both sides of the Atlantic. You'll need specific equipment, of course: Use large pots on stands over liquid or canned fuel burners to cook meat dishes. Smaller pots over candles can be used for cheeses and dessert sauces. If you have fondue forks, fine—or you may purchase inexpensive wooden bamboo skewers and simply replace them between courses.

Index

Order Form

Qty.	Title	Author	Order No.	Unit Cost (U.S. $)	Total
	Best Baby Shower Book	Cooke, Courtney	1239	$7.00	
	Best Baby Shower Party Games #1	Cooke, Courtney	6063	$3.95	
	Best Baby Shower Party Games #2	Cooke, Courtney	6069	$3.95	
	Best Bridal Shower Party Games #1	Cooke, Courtney	6060	$3.95	
	Best Bridal Shower Party Games #2	Cooke, Courtney	6068	$3.95	
	Best Party Book	Warner, Penny	6089	$9.00	
	Best Wedding Shower Book	Cooke, Courtney	6059	$7.00	
	Dinner Party Cookbook	Brown, Karen	6035	$9.00	
	Games People Play	Warner, Penny	6093	$8.00	
	Pick A Party	Sachs, Patty	6085	$9.00	
	Pick-A-Party Cookbook	Sachs, Patty	6086	$11.00	
	Something Old, Something New	Long, Becky	6011	$9.95	
	Storybook Weddings	Kring, Robin	6010	$8.00	
				Subtotal	
			Shipping and Handling (see below)		
			MN residents add 6.5% sales tax		
				Total	

YES! Please send me the books indicated above. Add $2.00 shipping and handling for the first book with a retail price up to $9.99. or $3.00 for the first book with a retail price of over $9.99. Add $1.00 shipping and handling for each additional book. All orders must be prepaid. Most orders are shipped within two days by U.S. Mail (7–9 delivery days). Rush shipping is available for an extra charge. Overseas postage will be billed. **Quantity discounts available upon request.**

Send book(s) to:

Name _____ Address _____

City _____ State _____ Zip _____

Telephone (_____)_____

Payment via:

❑ Check or money order payable to Meadowbrook Press (No cash or CODs please)

❑ Visa (for orders over $10.00 only)   ❑ MasterCard (for orders over $10.00 only)

Account # _____ Signature _____

Exp. Date _____

A *FREE* Meadowbrook Press catalog is available upon request.
You can also phone or fax us with a credit card order.

Mail to: Meadowbrook Press
5451 Smetana Drive, Minnetonka, MN 55343
Toll-Free 1-800-338-2232

Phone 612-930-1100   Fax 612-930-1940

For more information (and fun) visit our website:
www.meadowbrookpress.com